LEGAL ASPECTS OF REGULATORY TREATMENT OF BANKS IN DISTRESS

Tobias M.C. Asser

INTERNATIONAL MONETARY FUND

2001

Cover design: Lai Oy Louie
Composition: Jack Federici

Cataloging-in-Publication Data

Asser, T. M. C. (Tobias Michael Carel), 1935-
   Legal aspects of regulatory treatment of banks in distress / Tobias
M.C. Asser. _ Washington, D.C. : International Monetary Fund, 2001.

   p.   cm.

Includes bibliographical references.
ISBN 1-55775-972-3

1. Bank failures – Law and legislation. 2. Bankruptcy – Law and legisla-
tion. 3. Banking law. 4. Banks and banking – State supervision. I.
International Monetary Fund.
   HG1521.A77 2001

Price: $26.00

Please send orders to:
International Monetary Fund, Publication Services
700 19th Street, N.W., Washington, D.C. 20431, U.S.A.
Tel.: (202) 623-7430   Telefax: (202) 623-7201
E-mail: publications@imf.org
Internet: http://www.imf.org

recycled paper

Contents

Preface

This book is based on a comparative study of the law of selected countries with banking legislation that may serve as standard for the treatment of banks in distress. This report is consistent with and builds on the G-22 Working Group Reports on the International Financial Architecture, issued in October 1998, and the report on *Orderly and Effective Insolvency Procedures*: Key Issues, prepared by the Legal Department of the IMF and published in August 1999.

The author of this book is a former Assistant General Counsel of the IMF, who prepared it in close consultation with several bank insolvency experts, both inside and outside the IMF. Special thanks for their valuable assistance are extended to:

- Stephen Adamson (United Kingdom), a National Partner in charge of Restructuring Services of Ernst & Young and an advisor to the Government of the United Kingdom as a nonexecutive member of the Insolvency Services Executive Agency Steering Board;

- Ross Delston (United States), Attorney-at-Law and a former Assistant General Counsel of the Federal Deposit Insurance Corporation;

- Jordan Luke (United States), a partner in the law firm of Davis Polk & Wardwell and a former general counsel to the Federal Home Loan Bank Board.

Within the IMF's Legal Department, the support of François P. Gianviti and William E. Holder, the comments of Hermann W. Krull and Bernhard Steinki, and the assistance of Rachel Ray are gratefully acknowledged. The report has benefited greatly from the patient explanations of banking policy by Stefan N.M. Ingves, Warren Coats, and Marc G. Quintyn of the IMF's Monetary and Exchange Affairs Department, and the extensive comments and suggestions provided by Gudrun Mauerhofer of the Austrian National Bank, Glenn Hoggarth of the Bank of England, and Urs Zulauf and Eva Hüpkes of the Swiss Federal Banking Commission. David Driscoll edited the paper, and Gail Berre of the IMF External Relations Department coordinated production of the publication.

The opinions expressed in this report are those of the author and are not necessarily shared by the Executive Board or the staff of the IMF.

August 2000

Overview

During the last two decades, the deregulation of domestic and international banking transactions and the growth of national and international capital markets have had profound effects on the business of banking.

In many countries, domestic capital markets drew both borrowers and depositors away from banks, forcing banks to replace traditional forms of relationship banking with a broad array of financial services and to supplement their funding from traditional forms of deposit with funding from financial markets. These developments required a reappraisal of bank regulation and supervision to protect domestic financial sectors from the new systemic risks that they pose.

Banks have played a crucial international role in the unprecedented growth of cross-border capital flows, especially to emerging markets. This has led to a continuing financial integration of national economies, which has brought many benefits, including dramatic increases in global investment and consumption that have stimulated global trade and prosperity. However, there is a downside to this expansion of international banking activities: it has facilitated the spread of domestic financial problems throughout the international monetary system. By intermediating international capital flows, banks have created a global web of financial interests. This has made banks conduits for the transmission of domestic economic problems around the globe. Consequently, it has become more difficult than in the past to contain economic problems within the borders of the countries where they originate. Central to this transmission mechanism is the fact that many of a bank's foreign counterparties are banks. When weaknesses in one country's banking system translate into defaults on international financial obligations, the financial condition of creditor banks in other countries may be affected. Ultimately, this can cause a general loss of confidence on the part of investors and precipitate a steep fall in exchange rates and a national economic crisis. In some cases (*Indonesia, Russia*), the collapse of domestic banking systems worsened the effects of these crises, impeded debt workouts, and postponed the resumption of international capital flows to the countries concerned.

1

One of the lessons learned from these disasters is that building and maintaining the confidence of domestic and foreign investors requires a credible bank regulatory system that closely supervises banks, strictly enforces banking law, helps restore ailing banking institutions to financial health, and expeditiously expels insolvent banks from the financial system. Such regulatory pruning or weeding helps preserve and promote vigor and growth in a financial system. It removes incentives for weak institutions not to comply with prudential regulations and helps thereby to eliminate unfair competition resulting when noncompliance with prudential requirements permits banks to benefit from a lower regulatory cost base than banks that do comply.

Another lesson learned is that creditor banks share in the blame for economic crises in foreign debtor countries when their irresponsible lending practices contribute to the buildup of excessive external debt. Thus, in recent years, several international currency crises found part of their origin in excessive foreign currency loans by international banks to foreign corporations ill suited to hedge inherent foreign exchange risks or to foreign banking institutions plagued by serious structural weaknesses. Therefore, where banking supervision is intent on the avoidance of domestic financial crises and on containing the adverse effects of such crises on foreign banks, it should address not only the international borrowing but also the international lending practices of banking institutions.

Finally, experience has taught that effective prudential regulation of banks participating in an international monetary system of growing complexity requires internationally uniform prudential standards that are strictly enforced by qualified and autonomous bank regulators in close cooperation with their foreign counterparts.

Scope of the Report

This book discusses legal aspects of the regulatory treatment of banks[1] in distress. Banks in distress should be distinguished from banks

---

[1] For the purposes of this book, a "bank" is deemed to be an undertaking whose business is to receive deposits or other repayable funds from the public and to grant credits for its own account, following Article 1 of the *First European Council Directive of 12 December 1977 concerning credit institutions* (77/780/EEC) (Official Journal No. L 322/30 of 12/17/77) (hereinafter "First European Banking Directive"), reprinted in *Current Legal Issues Affecting Central Banks*, ed. by Robert C. Effros, Vol. 2 (Washington: International Monetary Fund), 1994, at p. 251. In addition, the meaning of the term "bank" includes any other financial institution that is regulated similarly to banks.

that are merely weak. "Banks in distress" are defined as banks that are not in compliance with prudential banking law.

This book's main objective is to analyze and to compare the laws of selected industrial countries that may be regarded as representative for different approaches to the treatment of banks in distress. As the book focuses on legal aspects, it addresses only those banking and economic policy issues required for a proper understanding of the banking law or the legal strategies, procedures, and practices that have evolved in the treatment of banking problems. In doing so, the book does not intend to take positions on banking or economic policy issues, except where these are questionable in light of legal principle or law.

To protect banks and banking systems against the risk of international financial contagion, bank regulators around the world have embarked on an extensive program of harmonizing prudential banking standards among countries and fostering closer cooperation between national bank regulators. Particularly notable are the Core Principles for Effective Banking Supervision issued by the Basle Committee on Banking Supervision in September 1997 (hereinafter "the Basle Core Principles") and the G-22 Working Group Reports on the International Financial Architecture, issued in October 1998. It is fair to say that, as a result, the principal licensing and prudential requirements written into national banking laws have reached a high degree of uniformity. One of the reasons for this success is that it has been comparatively easy to identify best practices for these requirements.

In contrast, little international uniformity of law or practice exists in the area of banking regulation governing the treatment of banks in distress. This area of banking regulation is marked by a rich variety of regimes. Although this book may discuss advantages and disadvantages of these regimes, it avoids rating them, mainly because each appears to reflect a distinct legal tradition defying a value judgment. The book does identify what may be regarded as essential best practices—in the form of principal objectives at the end of book sections—but only for such general norms as rise above these differences.

The book does not attempt to identify which of the practices described would be more or less suitable for countries in different stages of socioeconomic development. In theory, at least, such choices could be made. For instance, there may be practical reasons for avoiding judicial involvement in bank insolvency in countries with a weak or corrupt judiciary, in exchange for alternative procedures for the review of decisions of bank regulators, provided that such alternative procedures afford banks and bank creditors reasonable protection from regulatory abuse.

In the treatment of banks in distress, the concept of best practices is therefore perceived as a relative concept indicating that best practices differ from country to country, depend on a country's legal and other social traditions, and progress with a country's development: what is best for one country is not necessarily good for another.

The book addresses bank regulation by bank regulators. However, in countries with a bank deposit insurance agency, the responsibility for the prudential regulation of banks is often shared with the deposit insurance agency where the law gives that agency a role in the rescue or resolution of banks in distress. Therefore, generic references in this book to the bank regulator and to banking law are meant to include references to the deposit insurance agency and deposit insurance law.

In some countries, banks are permitted to engage in activities submitted to the prudential oversight of agencies other than the bank regulator, such as securities or insurance regulators and self-regulatory organizations. Usually, the law provides such agencies with their own regime of prudential supervision and powers to impose corrective measures or punitive sanctions. The book does not cover such measures and sanctions or the interaction between the bank regulator and such other agencies where it concerns laws or regulations that the other agencies are exclusively charged to enforce.

The book's conclusions and recommendations apply primarily to banks. They may, however, be applicable to other financial institutions. For instance, banks are not the only financial institutions to cause systemic risk that must be addressed. There have been instances in which support, usually preserved for banks, was extended to nonbank financial institutions whose precarious financial condition posed risks to the banking system; examples are the liquidity support provided to stock exchange specialists during the stock market crash of October 1987 in the United States and the meeting of creditors held under the auspices of the New York Federal Reserve Bank in the summer of 1998 to organize supplemental funding for the Long Term Capital Management hedge fund. For reasons of economy, this book does not address the treatment of nonbank financial institutions, even though some of the book's findings and conclusions may apply to those institutions as well.

This book begins where prudential enforcement gives way to corrective action. It is organized as a progression from noncompliance with prudential requirements and early signs of financial distress to insolvency, from relatively simple corrective measures to receivership culminating in revocation of the bank's operating license and closure of the bank.

The book has a domestic focus. There is no international bank regulator, as yet. Bank regulation and supervision, including the response to banking problems, is still largely a national endeavor. Even in the European Union, notwithstanding monetary union, the prudential supervision of financial institutions remains decentralized and is carried out by national agencies. This book assumes that corrective actions concerning banks with international activities are governed by rules of the Basle Committee of Bank Supervisors assigning responsibility for banking supervision among national regulators. It does not cover international aspects of bank insolvency.[2]

Forced Liquidation and Restructuring of Banks: Differences Between Bank Insolvency Law and General Insolvency Law

This book follows the report on Orderly and Effective Insolvency Procedures: Key Issues, of the Legal Department of the International Monetary Fund published in 1999 (hereinafter "the Insolvency Report"). Therefore, and because in many countries the forced liquidation of insolvent banks under receivership is subject to materially the same insolvency rules as other enterprises, this book does not cover in detail the rules and procedures governing the forced liquidation of insolvent banks. Often, however, the law makes exceptions for banks to the general insolvency law; the most important of these are discussed.[3] As in some countries insolvent banks may be submitted to a receivership including forced liquidation under the banking law, the book includes a brief discussion of this treatment.[4]

Although in many countries the general insolvency law includes general rehabilitation provisions that may apply to banks, the banking law of several countries also includes a special regime for the restructuring of banks, often under control of the bank regulator. Even though, in most of these countries, the broad policy objectives served by rehabilitation provisions of general insolvency law are similar to those pursued

---

[2] See on that topic: Mario Giovanoli, and Gregor Heinrich, eds., *International Bank Insolvencies: A Central Bank's Perspective* (The Hague: Kluwer Law International), 1999.

[3] See Chapter XIII, below.

[4] See Chapter XI, Section 4, below.

by special bank restructuring law, there are some fundamental differences between the restructuring of banks under the banking law and the rehabilitation of nonbank enterprises (hereinafter "enterprises") under general insolvency law.[5] These include the following.

The first and most obvious difference is that, as a rule, enterprise rehabilitation under general insolvency law is instituted by court order and is carried out under judicial administration. Bank restructuring, on the other hand, is generally instituted by the bank regulator pursuant to the banking law and carried out under its control, even though in many countries the most invasive aspects of bank restructuring are subject to judicial review or administration.

Restructuring under banking law is a broader concept than rehabilitation under general insolvency law, in both time and functional scope. Enterprise rehabilitation under general insolvency law typically commences only if the enterprise has been declared insolvent on the basis of strict statutory standards. Restructuring a bank, however, may begin at a much earlier stage with corrective measures ordered by the bank regulator as soon as the bank shows significant signs of noncompliance with prudential requirements, even though such corrective measures may end in a court-supervised insolvency procedure including a final effort to rehabilitate the bank under general insolvency law. In many countries, bank restructuring is part of a continuum ranging from regulatory enforcement of prudential law to receivership.

These differences between enterprise rehabilitation and bank restructuring have important consequences for the protection of rights of creditors and owners under the law. In a general insolvency procedure, these rights are protected by procedural safeguards written into the law and by judicial administration of rehabilitation and liquidation proceedings. In bank restructuring, however, fewer safeguards are available as most of it is carried out by the bank regulator without judicial administration. In several countries, the law grants the bank regulator sweeping powers to take corrective action as required to protect the banking system. And, even though the bank regulator and its agents, such as provisional administrators and receivers, are subject to principles of administrative law affording bank owners and creditors protection against regulatory abuse, the appeal afforded to bank owners and creditors of regulatory decisions is often time-consuming and does not suspend the regulatory decision under review. Moreover, even

---

[5] To avoid confusion, the term "rehabilitation" will generally not be applied to banks; instead, the term "bank restructuring" will be used throughout the book.

where such agents appointed by bank regulators are experienced and licensed insolvency practitioners, they will not always be familiar with administrative law.

Difficult questions of public policy arise when the public interest in a sound banking sector and the expeditious decommissioning of failing banks that this requires are weighed against the interests of bank owners and creditors and the need to afford a reasonable degree of protection of those interests under the law. These questions come to a head when a bank becomes insolvent and when measures designed for bank restructuring must be particularly intrusive; in several countries, the law requires the bank regulator at that point to turn the proceedings over to the courts for bank restructuring [6] and ultimately for liquidation of the bank under general insolvency law.

---

[6] *England* provides an example; see Section 8 of the Insolvency Act 1986, as amended, and the Banks (Administration Proceedings) Order 1989, which makes Part II of the Insolvency Act 1986 generally applicable to banks.

General Policy Considerations

1. Special Treatment of Banks

Unlike most nonfinancial corporations, in a market-based economy, banks are subject to a special regime of licensing, regulation, and supervision (hereinafter also "prudential regulation"). In a market-based economy, the function of banks differs from that of other enterprises, calling for special treatment of banks by the state.

When compared with the law that governs nonfinancial enterprises, prudential regulation of banks is special in its enforcement of prudential rules and its treatment of banking problems. Unlike nonfinancial enterprises, banks are normally subject to a complex and comprehensive system of rules and procedures authorizing the bank regulator to enforce prudential regulations, to take corrective action with respect to banks not in compliance with banking law, and ultimately to take control of banks threatened with failure.

In what respect are banks so different as to justify special treatment? Because of their traditional role of intermediation between short-term demand deposits and medium- and long-term loans, banks are vulnerable to a sudden loss of confidence in their financial soundness on the part of its depositors, causing a run on the bank. If a bank is unable to meet the demand for withdrawals and becomes illiquid, the public may lose confidence in other banks as well. The failure of one bank may affect the financial health of other banks that are counterparties of the failing institution. Interbank contagion and loss of public confidence can quickly snowball into panic runs on otherwise healthy banks, which may ultimately bring down the entire banking system. It may damage the financial condition of other financial institutions and may even impair the operations of the financial markets and payment and securities transfer systems. Thus, the failure of one or more individual banks may have effects that extend well beyond the financial

8

scope of their operations. Moreover, a national banking crisis is difficult to contain within the borders of the country where it originates: owing to growing international business connections between banks of different countries, a banking crisis in one country can trigger a banking crisis in another.

Modern market economies cannot function properly without an efficient banking system intermediating between public savings and investments and providing other essential financial services to the public. Modern market economies cannot function properly without efficient financial markets or payment and securities transfer systems that depend on banking services. A sound banking system is necessary for the conduct of monetary policy and for the operation of payment systems. Prudential licensing and supervision of banks is dictated by these considerations and by concern for the safety of public savings deposited with banks; in countries with public deposit insurance, there is a need to protect the interests of the deposit insurance agency and indirectly the state treasury that may guarantee its solvency. Therefore, banks should receive special treatment and should be submitted to prudential regulation that aims at their safety and soundness.

Banking regulation includes the institutional supervision of banks in order to ensure compliance with prudential banking standards. Although, in practice, banking supervision is meant to help maintain the safety and soundness of each bank on an individual basis, the most compelling reason for prudential banking regulation is concern for the safety and soundness of the banking system as a whole, and ultimately of the national economy. Even the objective of protecting public savings is inspired not only by social goals but also by the fear that loss of public confidence would lead to wholesale withdrawals of savings from the banking system. Therefore, as prudential banking regulation finds its justification in the need to protect the banking system, the treatment of individual banks by the bank regulator must essentially be driven by systemic considerations and not necessarily by the interests of individual banks.

The foregoing argument does not mean that banks whose failure would not pose a risk to the banking system, e.g., owing to their relatively modest size or position in the national economy, could be exempt from banking regulation. Even if it could be argued in theory that there are such banks, it would in practice be difficult to determine *ex ante* whether or not the failure of these banks at some future moment would trigger a banking panic. It would be even more difficult to define the objective and uniform standards that would be needed to maintain equality of treatment among banks in deciding which bank should and which bank should not be exempt from banking regulation. Furthermore, it would be improper to exempt only some banks from prudential regulation, as unregulated banks would benefit from a lower regulatory cost base than banks subject to prudential regulation. Because regulatory exemptions would expose regulated banks to unfair competition from unregulated banks, the bank regulator must instead maintain a level regulatory playing field where similar banking activities carry similar regulatory burdens for all banks alike. Finally, even if it were possible to identify in the abstract banks that would individually be too unimportant to pose a risk to the banking system, the possibility that a significant number of such banks would fail could well pose a systemic risk, as is illustrated by the small bank crisis in *England* in the early 1990s.

The conclusion that banking supervision should essentially be driven by systemic considerations has important implications for the regulatory treatment of individual banks in distress. The interests of the banking system and the interests of individual banks do not always coincide. For systemic reasons, the bank regulator will permit some banks to fail. Regulatory action taken and the costs incurred by the authorities to rescue banking enterprises whose failure could not reasonably be expected to pose a threat to the banking system could not be justified on systemic grounds.[7] Actually, letting such banks fail would be in the interest of the banking system, because it would drive home to the owners and managers of other banks that unsafe or unsound banking practices have a price; this would help combat the systemic risk and moral hazard that the expectation of an official rescue would tempt banks to engage in improper banking activities.

An important legal issue to be addressed is whether the before-mentioned systemic reasons for the special treatment of banks are so strong as to justify exceptions for banks to the principle of judicial administration of the rehabilitation and winding up of insolvent institutions under general insolvency law. An extrajudicial regulatory process offers greater efficiency than a court-administered process; this is an important advantage if immediate action to close or transfer the business of a bank is required for systemic reasons. However, granting the regulator the power to act expeditiously and to avoid delays inher-

---

[7] The difficulties noted before in predicting whether the failure of a particular bank would or would not lead to systemic problems decrease as the time of prediction approaches the time of bank failure; here, the systemic effects of a bank failure are assessed when the bank failure occurs.

ent in court administration has a significant cost: excluding the courts tends to deprive bank creditors and other interested parties of the procedural and substantive safeguards that they enjoy under a proper court-administered proceeding. This argument carries even greater weight in bank insolvencies where the deposit insurance agency is appointed as receiver, as the agency will usually suffer a conflict between its interests as one of the largest creditors of the bank and its role as impartial receiver. These and other aspects of the regulatory takeover of banks are discussed below.[8]

2. Institutional Framework

Although, in most countries, dealing with banks in distress is first and foremost the responsibility of the bank regulator, other institutions may eventually be involved, such as the deposit insurance agency, bank restructuring corporations,[9] and the judiciary.

Nonbank financial institutions play an increasingly important role as custodians of public savings (brokerage houses, life insurance companies, pension funds, and mutual investment funds), and hence the effects that their failure may have on public wealth and on the financial system become increasingly significant. Therefore, in many countries, nonbank institutions are subject to prudential requirements and oversight, while some countries consolidate the prudential regulation of banks and other financial institutions under the roof of a single regulatory agency (*Australia, England, Japan, Korea, Norway, Sweden*).

To be effective, corrective action must be fair, swift, and decisive. This requires a bank regulator that is autonomous (i.e., financially and operationally independent from outside interference, accountable to the public, transparent and predictable in its regulatory activities of general application, and staffed with sufficient qualified and experienced personnel).

Accountability requires that the various prudential duties are assigned to a single authority for each bank or category of banks. In some countries, prudential responsibilities are divided between several agencies; typically, the issuance and revocation of banking licenses

---

[8] See Chapter VIII, Section 4, below, for a discussion of judicial administration. See Chapter VIII, Section 3 for a brief discussion of the role of deposit insurance agencies.

[9] Bank restructuring corporations are public agencies entrusted with the restructuring and liquidation of insolvent banks during a systemic banking crisis. They are discussed in Chapter XIV, below.

may be the responsibility of the minister of finance, while supervision of banks is entrusted to the central bank or another bank regulator such as the deposit insurance agency. Although such arrangements may be satisfactory for countries with a strong tradition of interagency cooperation (*United States*), in others they tend to promote negligent forbearance and to weaken accountability by giving each of the authorities an excuse for pointing the finger at the other when a bank fails.[10]

Transparency of policy and predictability of supervisory decision making are key characteristics of a good bank supervisory system: they help ensure equality of treatment among banks. An important contribution to transparency is made by submitting draft banking regulations to public comment before their final adoption and by rendering all regulatory decisions in rational and impartial judgment. Care should be exercised in publishing regulatory decisions affecting banks on an individual basis: if the market is unaware of a bank's difficulties, an announcement by the authorities that corrective action is being taken with respect to that bank may cause an adverse market reaction. Essential is the prompt publication of all prudential regulations and regulatory decisions that are of general application. Predictability of regulatory decisions is achieved when generally similar regulatory issues lead to similar regulatory decisions; reducing the risk of unexpected regulatory action tends to reduce transaction costs and to enhance the efficiency of the banking industry.

Obviously, banking supervision should be conducted on the basis of technical criteria without political consideration and without outside interference from the political establishment or lobbyists. The requirement of financial independence for the regulator is designed to avoid the risk of political influence peddling in exchange for financial support. Financial independence can be assured by assigning banking supervision to an autonomous central bank. For an independent supervision agency, financial autonomy can be built on levies from the banking industry and on the assumption that banks that meet prudential requirements have a strong interest in the enforcement of banking law against banks whose noncompliance exposes them to unfair competition.

---

[10] Similar problems may arise when institutional and functional supervision are carried out by different regulators and some banking activities are regulated by regulators other than the bank regulator, unless the different areas of regulatory jurisdiction and responsibility are clearly delineated by the law.

Wherever bank owners and managers have powerful political connections, quick and effective corrective action by the bank regulator is the true test of its autonomy. They are also a true test of the political will to maintain an effective bank regulatory framework, because the bank regulator operates by the grace of the legislature and cannot properly fulfill its task without political respect for regulatory autonomy. In countries with a powerful body politic and a relatively short tradition of independent state agencies, the autonomy of the bank regulator may be strengthened by providing for judicial or administrative review of its decisions, as such review offers bank managers and owners a forum for grievances and politicians an excuse for staying on the sidelines.

The need to keep the political establishment out of decisions concerning individual banks sounds more obvious than it really is, especially where such banks occupy a central position in the national economy. On the one hand, it is clear that prudential bank regulation should be based on bank-technical standards. On the other hand, banking supervision is a public function that, if deficient, tends to cause great harm to the nation; it is understandable, therefore, that the body politic wishes to be involved beyond its legislative function. A balance can be struck between these interests by granting the government control over appointments to the decision-making organs of the bank regulator without impairing the regulator's functional autonomy.[11]

3. Incidental Versus Banking System Problems

In discussing the modalities of banking regulation, it is useful to distinguish between "normal" situations where a banking system is reasonably sound and bank failures occur only sporadically on an incidental basis and the exceptional situation where a country suffers from an economic crisis of such magnitude as to threaten the failure of the entire banking system. Systemic banking crises, such as those recently encountered in *Asia* and *Russia*, commonly require exceptionally strong corrective measures designed to restore confidence in the financial markets quickly.

---

[11] In *France*, the Banking Commission provides an example of such an institutional arrangement—Article 38 of Law No. 84-46 of January 24, 1984, on the Activities and Supervision of Credit Institutions. The Commission's membership includes the Governor of the central bank or his representative as chairman, the Director of the Treasury or his representative, a member of the Council of State, a judge of the *Cour de Cassation* (the highest civil court), and two other members selected on the basis of their expertise in banking and financial matters.

Accordingly, the book distinguishes between incidental banking problems and systemic banking crises. Although regulators may use powers granted for incidental cases also in crisis situations, systemic banking crises require additional strategies and super powers that would generally not be justified in "normal" situations. Systemic banking crises are addressed in the final section of this book.

4. The Corrective Effects of Market Forces

Because banks operating in market-based economies are exposed to the financial markets (including other banks) for their funding and other financial activities, they are subject to the vagaries of the market place. At the same time, banks are subject to prudential regulation including corrective action imposed by the banking supervisor, which in a sense interferes with the market place. This section of the book offers a brief discussion of some of the considerations that go into seeking a proper balance between the corrective effect of market forces and the corrective effect of regulatory action on banks.

In a market economy, market forces largely determine the terms and conditions on which market participants compete with each other. One of the risks of regulatory intervention is that by altering those terms and conditions it may distort or impede competition between banks and stifle banking product innovation; hence the need for a proper balance between market forces and regulation.[12]

Financial markets tend to correct errors in judgment and thereby impose discipline on market participants. Thus, for instance, when weak banks are permitted to succumb to market forces, the risk of bank failure provides a powerful incentive for bank owners and managers to keep their institutions safe and sound. Conversely, placing regulatory constraints on the corrective effects of market forces (e.g., by preventing banks from failing through regulatory intervention) weakens the discipline imposed by the market place.

---

[12] This risk occurs not only at the macroeconomic level—for instance, as a result of excessive regulation—but also with respect to the competitive relationships between individual banks—for instance, when a failing bank is the beneficiary of operational or financial assistance from the authorities without paying its cost and thereby enjoys a competitive advantage over other banks. As a result, banks that do comply with prudential standards are not penalized by unfair competition from banks that do not. Because such unfair competition produces harmful economic distortions, bank regulators generally try to maintain a level playing field for banks where the costs of prudential regulation apply equally and ratably to all banks.

It can be readily admitted that it is not the task of the bank regulator to try and save every bank that is threatened by demise. Bank failure should not be treated as an abnormal event and prudential bank regulation should certainly not be expected to guarantee the safety and soundness of each and every bank. As a general proposition, banks do fail and should be allowed to fail.

There are times, however, where economic conditions are so severe that they threaten the entire banking system. For instance, in the Asian crisis of 1997 such systemic threats resulted from unexpected changes in exogenous economic conditions followed by exceptionally strong reactions on the part of bank depositors and other providers of funds to what the financial markets perceive as significant weaknesses in one or more important banks or the banking system as a whole. As market economies cannot function properly without a banking system, the bank regulator must step in to protect the banking system against such threats. In doing so, the bank regulator must calibrate the extent of its regulatory intervention in banking operations so as to strike a proper balance between, on the one hand, preventing bank failures that would significantly and adversely affect the public confidence in the banking system and, on the other hand, promoting competition and innovation in the banking sector. Finding and maintaining such balance belongs to the most difficult tasks of the bank regulator.

The deregulation of banking operations combined with the communications revolution and the resulting fundamental changes in banking activities have made this task even harder. For example, much of the threat to banking systems caused by market forces results from markets overreacting to negative news. With the shift in their funding from insured private individuals to uninsured sophisticated financial institutions, and the shift from traditional loan-based banking operations to trade- and service-based banking activities, banks have become more exposed to market judgments about the risks that they pose to their counterparties. In addition, the exponential growth in foreign exchange and derivatives operations of large banks with other financial institutions has made them more vulnerable to price volatility and real or perceived adverse changes in their financial condition. Uninsured financial institutions react faster and more forcefully to unexpected negative news concerning a bank counterparty than insured household depositors. By increasing the speed with which information is disseminated, financial judgments are arrived at, and investment decisions are taken, the communications revolution has added to the volatility of market sentiment.

What can be done in this environment to avoid excessive market reactions to banking problems, and thereby to mitigate their destructive effects on the banking system as a whole, without reversing the deregulation of the banking industry? The first line of defense is adequate prudential regulation of banks by a regulator enjoying public trust. The second has traditionally been deposit insurance in one form or another. The third would be the timely publication of adequate and transparent information concerning individual banks, especially where they warn the financial markets about impending problems of banks at a time when the problems are still relatively small and the markets therefore may be expected to react to them with restraint.

The more sophisticated financial market participants are, the more they will benefit from improved bank information flows. Better financial reporting will serve the interests not only of bank counterparties but also of the banks themselves. Although it might at first glance appear that greater timeliness and transparency in financial reporting by banks would make their market position more volatile, this timeliness and transparency would actually help smooth reactions of bank counterparties and help protect banks against damaging market action driven by unfounded rumor.

For household depositors with banks, the situation appears to be different. Better financial reporting by banks would affect the behavior of household depositors only if such reporting becomes more consumer friendly. For them, greater transparency in financial reporting should entail not only greater quantities of timely financial data, but also, and especially, drastic improvements in the presentation of such data. Currently, the information advantage of sophisticated investors over unsophisticated household depositors not only consists of better access to more complete information—although the internet is rapidly bridging this gap—but concerns mainly the ability to digest and use that information. Before unsophisticated household depositors can reasonably be expected to play a useful role in imposing market discipline on banks, the financial information concerning banks that is needed to make regularly informed judgments about a bank's safety and soundness must be presented in a format that can readily be understood by the general public. This requires both changes in the presentation of financial information and education of the public in absorbing and using that information. Until such changes have been carried out, generally unsophisticated household depositors cannot be expected to make adequate or timely judgments about the soundness of the institutions where they bank, except in extreme cases.

This judgment concerning household depositors is borne out by the fact that runs on banks by depositors typically have come too late—namely, when the bank concerned was already on the brink of failure—or too early, when contagion led to panic runs on banks that were sound. Providing more information about banks may not be helpful either. In fact, negative market signals have had the perverse effect of attracting depositors instead of repelling them, such as when depositors were prompted to move their money into a bank offering relatively high deposit rates, without realizing that these attractive rates compensated for a higher risk of failure resulting from weaknesses in the bank's financial condition.[13] Therefore, household depositors should generally not yet be relied on to provide a gradual response to gradual changes in the financial condition of their banks. This may change as the financial literacy of the general public improves, and indeed, one of the objectives of banking regulation should be to promote public knowledge and understanding of the banking system and thereby to improve the ability of household depositors to form adequate judgments about the safety and soundness of their banking institutions. Meanwhile, deposit insurance may be used to protect the banking system against depositor-led banking panics.[14]

The corrective effects of market forces present bank regulators with a dilemma. On the one hand, the discipline that the financial marketplace imposes by penalizing a bank's deficiencies in the form of lower credit ratings and higher interest or collateral requirements alleviates the task of the regulator. On the other hand, the increased risk of excessive market reactions makes the regulator's task more difficult. In a market environment, corrective action taken by the bank regulator to strengthen a bank's financial condition may be interpreted in the market as evidence of serious problems and have the unintended effect of causing an adverse market reaction that increases the bank's cost of funding and thereby weakens the bank even further, triggering the very chain of events that corrective action is designed to fore-

---

[13] Not only unsophisticated household depositors fall into this trap. Similar mistakes were repeatedly made by sophisticated international investors who were attracted by relatively high interest rates in countries that for some time had successfully maintained stable exchange rates for their currencies, with little or no regard to the fact that exchange stability was bought at the price of relatively high domestic interest rates, masking serious macroeconomic weaknesses.

[14] Of course, deposit insurance may perversely cause complacency among household depositors about the financial condition of their banks, especially if the insurance cover is generous.

stall.[15] It may even raise the specter of contagion of other banks. Although this risk should never serve as an excuse for regulatory forbearance, it does raise questions concerning the manner in which regulatory corrective action is taken. And it strongly supports the conclusion that bank regulation should be market sensitive.

Ideally, the bank regulator maintains a proper balance between the corrective effect of market forces and regulatory intervention, limiting regulatory constraints on market forces to situations where this is clearly justified by systemic considerations.

Deposit insurance adds a wrinkle to this line of reasoning, as it provides a disincentive for depositors to withdraw their funds from a bank when the financial health of the bank deteriorates. Consequently, bank managers are tempted to engage in unsound banking practices, in the expectation that because of deposit insurance such practices will not cause depositors to leave the bank, creating a condition known as "moral hazard." For small banks, the moral hazard implicit in deposit insurance can be countered by the strict enforcement of explicit exit policies for failing banks. For larger banks relying on the financial markets for much of their funding and income, moral hazard implicit in deposit insurance is reduced by their exposure to the corrective effects of market forces.

Unfortunately, other factors also cause moral hazard. For banks deemed indispensable to the proper operation of the banking system, the financial markets, including the banks themselves, tend to assume that the banks will be bailed out by the monetary authorities. This judgment is generally made *ex ante*, long before the first signs of trouble. The possibility, or rather the probability, that such banks will be rescued because they would be "too big to fail"[16] exposes society to the moral hazard that bank owners and managers may be encouraged to engage in unsound banking practices. It is difficult to measure the influence of this implicit guarantee on the cost of operations of such banks, or the effects of such thinking on the behavior of their managers and owners. There is evidence that it is conducive to a go-for-broke mentality, tempting bank managers and owners to take ever

---

[15] This assumes, of course, that the markets discover in one way or another the corrective activities of the regulator. In most developed markets, that assumption is not unreasonable.

[16] The term "too big to fail" is imprecise. Meant are not only banks the size of whose business is so large that its failure would place the banking system at risk, but also *inter alia* smaller banks that have a key position in the banking system, and banks that are too large to wind down in an orderly fashion rather than too big to fail *per se*.

greater risks as bank capital erodes, shifting the risk of loss to the monetary authorities,[17] especially in countries where the law does not threaten such reckless behavior with effective civil or criminal penalties. Meanwhile, it is not difficult to see how the assumption that such a guarantee exists can lead to complacency on the part of investors and blunt the corrective effects of market forces. But, would such investor confidence—even though misplaced—not tend to protect such a bank from adverse market action? Initially it may indeed. Ultimately, however, as the bank's financial condition continues to deteriorate, the market will begin to question its own assumptions about the existence of a guarantee for that bank and, when it is not explicitly confirmed by the authorities, react with even greater force than before.

In *England*, the Financial Services and Markets Act 2000 condenses the foregoing to three statutory objectives of financial regulation that the Financial Services Authority (FSA) as regulator must so far as is reasonably possible comply with: market confidence, public awareness, and the protection of consumers.[18] The Act defines these regulatory objectives as follows: *the market confidence objective* is maintaining confidence in the financial system (including banking activities); *the public awareness objective* is promoting public understanding of the financial system, including, in particular, promoting awareness of the benefits and risks associated with different kinds of investment or other financial dealing, and the provision of appropriate information and advice; and *the protection of consumers objective* is securing the appropriate degree of protection for consumers.[19] In addition, the Act requires that the FSA, in discharging its general functions, must have regard to several principles of good regulation, which include the following (as translated for banks):

---

[17] Richard J. Herring, "Banking Disasters: Causes and Preventive Measures, Lessons Derived from the U.S. Experience" in *Preventing Bank Crises: Lessons from Recent Global Bank Failures*, ed. by Caprio, Hunter, Kaufman, and Leipziger (Washington, World Bank), 1998, p. 209 at p. 224.

[18] Section 2 of the Act; the other regulatory objective specified by the Act is the reduction of financial crime.

[19] Sections 3 to 5 of the Financial Services and Markets Act 2000. Broadly speaking, with respect to banks, consumers are persons using banking services and persons having rights attributable to or adversely affected by the use of banking services by other persons—Section 138(7) of the Act. In considering what degree of consumer protection may be appropriate with respect to bank activities, the FSA must have regard to the differing degrees of risk involved in different kinds of investment or other transaction, the differing degrees of experience and expertise of different consumers in relation to different kinds of banking activity, the needs that consumers may have for advice and accurate information, and the general principle that consumers should take responsibility for their decisions—Section 5(2) of the Act.

- the principle that a burden or restriction which is imposed on a person, or on the carrying on of an activity, should be proportionate to the benefits, considered in general terms, which are expected to result from the imposition of that burden or restriction;
- the desirability of facilitating innovation in connection with banking activities; the need to minimize the adverse effects on competition that may arise from anything done in the discharge of those functions; and the desirability of facilitating competition between banks.[20]

5. Liquidity Support Provided by the Central Bank as Lender of Last Resort

Just like other institutions, banks must ensure that they are able to meet their liabilities as these become due. However, compared with other companies, banks face special difficulties in meeting this requirement. Traditionally, banks use funds received by them mainly in the form of demand deposits and unsecured short-term borrowings in the financial markets to make medium- to long-term loans. The resulting mismatch between the maturities of a bank's loan assets and its funding liabilities requires a bank to manage its resources with care so that it has sufficient liquid resources[21] to meet its current payment obligations. Accordingly, prudential banking regulations usually require banks to maintain certain minimum levels of liquid resources that are measured as a fraction of their short-term obligations or that observe certain maximum time spreads between maturity classes of assets and liabilities.[22]

Several sources of funds and techniques are available to banks to supplement their liquid resources. In the major industrial countries, banks have access to money markets, including the interbank market, for overnight borrowing under arrangements that may include loans secured by collateral or security repurchase agreements. In addition, banks that are account holders with their central bank usually have

---

[20] Section 2(3) of the Financial Services and Markets Act 2000.

[21] Liquid resources are understood to include not only cash and deposit balances payable on demand but also other assets that can be sold immediately for a reasonable price.

[22] See Basle Committee on Banking Supervision, *A Framework for Measuring and Managing Liquidity* (Basel: Bank for International Settlements), September 1992.

access to the central bank's discount or lombard loan window or to overdraft facilities under payment, clearing, and settlement systems operated by the central bank. Often, however, central bank funding is subject to restrictions or collateral requirements. The law typically pre-scribes which types of assets are eligible for central bank discounting or collateral. And financial assistance by the central bank is nearly always subject to the condition that it is compatible with the central bank's monetary policy stance, although exceptionally financial assistance may also be granted otherwise if its monetary effects are sterilized.

Sometimes, however, banks are confronted with unforeseen devel-opments that close their access to ordinary sources of funds, threaten-ing their ability to continue meeting their liabilities as these fall due. This may be caused by unusual changes in the macroeconomic envi-ronment in which banks operate and over which they have little or no control. A typical example would be an unexpected loss of public con-fidence in the banking system, triggered perhaps by a currency crisis or the failure of another financial institution. Such an event may close access of the bank to the interbank market and eventually cause a depositor run on the bank. It is in such situations, where a bank expe-riences a catastrophic liquidity shortfall, that the question arises whether an otherwise solvent bank should be allowed to fall victim to market forces beyond its control, just as most nonbank enterprises would be allowed to fail, or whether the authorities should step in to meet the bank's short-term liquidity needs.

As was said before, prudential regulation of banks is not designed to eliminate all bank failures. Banks engage in a risky business, and it should be expected that some will fail. The question is therefore not whether banks should be allowed to fail—many clearly should—but whether a particular bank should be allowed to fail or whether it should receive lender-of-last-resort support from the central bank. The answer to this question generally depends on a judgment whether the failure of that bank would imperil the integrity of the banking sys-tem—for instance, because its failure must be expected to cause a run on other banks or because the bank is judged an essential component of the country's financial sector. In answering the question, a distinc-tion should be drawn between the needs of a failing bank and the needs of the banking system as a whole.

Lender-of-last-resort support to a failing bank is traditionally under-stood to consist of liquidity support in the form of a collateralized loan provided in exceptional circumstances by the central bank to the fail-ing bank if the failing bank is still solvent. Liquidity support may take other forms or be provided by another agency, however. For instance, it may be provided in the form of a central bank deposit of funds with the bank. In countries with deposit insurance, the deposit insurance agency is often authorized by law to provide liquidity support to insured banking institutions, ostensibly to reduce the risk of loss to the agency.[23]

Lender-of-last-resort assistance is exceptional. Therefore, it must be distinguished from liquidity support provided by the central bank to the banking system through normal channels, such as lombard and discount windows.

As lender-of-last-resort assistance, by definition, is available only to solvent banks, it must also be distinguished from exceptional financial support, or "open bank assistance" as it is sometimes called, which is provided to banks that are insolvent.[24] In practice, however, the urgency of the situation may prevent the central bank from reaching a reliable judgment concerning the bank's solvency. Lender-of-last-resort financing from the central bank is usually available only when the problems causing the liquidity shortfall are expected to be of a short duration and where the bank, notwithstanding its lack of liquidity, is still solvent, i.e., where the bank's assets have a value that exceeds the aggregate nominal amount of the bank's liabilities.[25] If the bank is insolvent, it would usually not be eligible for central bank funding, and financial assistance must come from the government. Often, the true financial condition of an illiquid bank cannot be ascertained and the risk that the bank would prove to be insolvent cannot be properly assessed without spending time on a bank audit that the urgency of the situation does not allow. Therefore, it is suggested that the burden of proof of insolvency be turned around so that banks requesting lender-of-last-resort assistance would be presumed to be insolvent, unless they prove otherwise.[26]

Other practical difficulties must be perhaps overcome before lender-of-last-resort support may be made available. In a desperate attempt to

---

[23] E.g., *Austria*: Article 93a(6) of the Austrian Banking Act; *Canada*: Section 10(1) of the Canada Deposit Insurance Corporation Act; *United States*: 12 U.S.C. § 1823(c)(1).

[24] See Chapter VI, below, for a discussion of exceptional financial support to insolvent banks.

[25] Conversely, a bank is generally deemed insolvent when the value of its assets is less than the aggregate nominal amount of its liabilities. Often, the bank supervisor uses the concept of regulatory insolvency, which measures solvency in terms of the adequacy of a bank's capital to meet prudential standards.

[26] Indeed, experience teaches that banks that can no longer meet their liquidity needs through traditional channels of funding are usually not only illiquid but also insolvent.

obtain liquid resources, the bank may have sold most of its assets that the central bank could otherwise have accepted as collateral for credit to the bank. Or, conversely, if assets that could serve as security for central bank credit are still available, the bank may be committed under negative pledge covenants with its existing lenders not to grant any collateral to new lenders, or under *pari passu* covenants to ensure that existing lenders share in or are given collateral equivalent to the collateral granted to new lenders; in any event, the aggregate principal amount outstanding on the bank's debt will often exceed the combined value of those of its assets that could serve as collateral. If negative pledge or *pari passu* covenants are obstacles to the provision of collateral, the central bank may be able to buy assets from the bank, if necessary through a special intermediary created for the purpose, before they are securitized and marketed.[27] Another technique for circumventing the prohibition on central bank lending to the bank without adequate collateral is for the central bank to make a loan to the state for onlending by the state to the bank in distress; the central bank loan to the state may be collateralized by, or take the form of a sale to the central bank of, marketable government securities bearing interest at market rates.

If a bank is assumed or found to be insolvent or if it cannot offer eligible collateral, it must be decided whether the bank should nevertheless receive exceptional liquidity support from the state treasury or from another official source, such as the deposit insurance agency. In addition, regardless of whether lender-of-last-resort support is provided or withheld, the central bank may add liquidity to the banking system as a whole in order to stave off depositors' runs on other banks and thereby to contain the adverse systemic effects of a bank failure.

Although, under banking law, liquidity support is often treated independently from other regulatory measures, usually such support would be linked to a plan of bank restructuring designed to return the bank to a condition where support is no longer needed to service its obligations. It stands to reason that the rate of interest and other fees charged by the monetary authorities in exchange for such emergency assistance should be high enough to reflect the risks associated with the rescue operation and to exclude that, owing to public assistance, the stake of the bank's owners would improve without penalty (free ridership).

---

[27] See for this technique: Stefan Gannon, "The Use of Securitization to Mobilize Liquidity and in Particular the Use of Specialized Mortgage Corporations," in *International Bank Insolvencies: A Central Bank's Perspective*, ed. by Mario Giovanoli and Gregor Heinrich (The Hague: Kluwer Law International), 1999, p. 301 at p. 309.

In practice, however, the rate of interest and other fees charged are rarely adequate—if they were, the bank could have obtained market funding on those terms. It may be preferable, therefore, to penalize bank managers by removing them (unless the bank's difficulties are due to circumstances beyond their control) and to ensure that bank owners bear the full cost of support, including penalties where appropriate—for instance, by suspending dividend payments until the cost has been paid out of the bank's net revenues.

In some countries, official liquidity support comes indirectly when the law authorizes the bank regulator to declare a moratorium and to suspend some or all of the debt-service payments to be made by the bank. In this manner, liquid resources are freed up—resources that the bank otherwise would have needed to meet its obligations—permitting the bank to ride out the storm or to arrange a debt workout with its creditors.[28]

For central banks responsible for banking supervision, lender-of-last-resort assistance may carry political costs. There may be fear that the central bank would misuse its lender-of-last-resort facility to cover up its own deficient prudential oversight. And, once financial assistance has been provided by the central bank, it will often saddle the central bank with a large loan asset of doubtful value that is collateralized by questionable assets; this may make it difficult for the central bank to support closing the bank and swallowing the resulting loss. These are among the considerations that have been advanced for assigning the task of banking supervision to an agency other than the central bank.

6. Prevention

The principal objective of prudential regulation of banks is to maintain a sound banking system. To achieve this objective, an effective system and a suitable legal framework for banking supervision will be required, meeting the standards set out in the Basle Core Principles. In this sense, enforcement of banking law and the regulatory intervention discussed in this book all aim at preventing banking problems.

However, these goals cannot be reached without a culture that fosters voluntary compliance with prudential requirements on the part of bank owners and management: it is practically impossible to place a bank regulator behind the chair of every bank manager.

---

[28] See Chapter VII for a discussion of debt service moratoria.

In addition, several external conditions are conducive to a sound banking system. These include in particular the following:

- a strong legal framework providing banks certainty concerning their rights and obligations under the law and permitting them to enforce their financial claims expeditiously and effectively against counterparties in default;[29]

- a proper corporate framework for banks[30] that is characterized by good governance, adequate internal risk management and financial control systems, market-based decision-making, and respect for shareholders' rights;

- proper incentives and disincentives for bank owners, managers, and directors, ranging from the effects of market forces on the bank's financial position to personal liability for gross negligence and willful misconduct;[31]

- regular publication of informative financial statements drawn up in accordance with internationally accepted accounting practices and audited by qualified and independent external auditors, promoting sound market judgments;

- adequate payment, clearing, and settlement systems for transfers of money and securities; and

- efficient financial markets that not only enable banks to meet their ordinary liquidity needs and to calibrate their overall risk profile by disposing of assets and hedging liabilities, but also support reasonable asset valuations for accounting and risk management purposes.

Finally, no banking system can function properly without public trust. Therefore, an important objective of the prudential regulation of banks is to build and maintain public confidence in the banking system. This objective is pursued not only by the issue and enforcement of prudential regulations but also by educating the public about the banking industry. Such education should include explaining to the

---

[29] See Chapter II, Section 1, below.

[30] Weaknesses in the general corporate framework, e.g., in the company law, may be addressed and corrected for banks in the banking law.

[31] Several countries place stock in the preventive force of civil or criminal penalties imposed by the bank regulator, or by a court upon the application of the regulator, and especially the embarrassment caused for a bank by their publication. See *Belgium*: Article 104 of the Law on the Statute and Supervision of Credit Institutions; *England*: Sections 44, 81, and 94 of the Banking Act 1987; *France*: Articles 75 ff. of Law No. 84-46 on the Activities and Supervision of Credit Institutions; *Germany*: Articles 54–59 of the Law on the Credit System.

public the risks of banking and the prudential standards applied to mitigate those risks, publishing important decisions of the bank regulator, and fostering reasonable expectations among the public about the continuing safety and soundness of banks. Most important is that the bank regulator has public credibility. Credibility of the bank regulator is enhanced by granting the bank regulator autonomy of decision making, by a transparent and uniform application of prudential regulations and policies, and by a proper, timely, and decisive response to banking problems.

II

General Legal Considerations

1. The Law Governing Banking Activities

Banks require a strong legal framework providing certainty concerning their rights and obligations under the law and permitting them to enforce their financial claims expeditiously and effectively against counterparties in default. Conversely, weaknesses in the legal system that create uncertainties concerning the existence and enforceability of property rights increase the risk that, as debtors hiding behind such weaknesses default on their obligations, banks will not be able to collect on their claims. Inefficiencies in the judicial processing of financial claims by banks may inhibit the marketing of financial assets and reduce their value; this often results in unhealthy accumulations of nonperforming assets on banks' balance sheets, weakening the banking system as a whole. Meanwhile, banks will cover these risks and market inefficiencies in the form of higher charges, creating upward pressure on transaction costs throughout the economy.

Not only do weaknesses in the law tend to weaken banks by reducing the value of their financial assets, but systemic legal deficiencies stand in the way of successful corrective action aimed at restoring financial health in banks; and, for banks in liquidation, these deficiencies impede the marketing of financial assets against reasonable prices.

Even seemingly minor procedural weaknesses in a legal system can have far-reaching economic consequences. For instance, in one country, where the law requires creditors to process foreclosure auctions of real estate mortgages through the courts, delays in court proceedings and in the payment of the auction proceeds to creditor-mortgagees effectively blocked the development of a real estate loan market.[32]

---

[32] This has consequences for financial system stability assessments carried out by the IMF. Surveillance of the financial sector of a country cannot be complete without surveillance of its legal framework. Surveillance of the legal framework of a country must focus not merely on the letter of the law but also and especially on the practice of the law and the degree to which it promotes the efficient discharge of financial obligations.

Although there is a good deal of international uniformity of banking law and regulations governing the legal status, organization, and operations of banks, there is less agreement in the area of banking law governing regulatory corrective action and bank receivership. There are considerable differences in national regimes where it concerns the treatment of banks that do not respond to corrective measures ordered by the regulator and which are brought under the regulator's control, in order to save part or all of a bank's business, or to merge it with another institution, or to close the bank. As was noted before, one of the issues for which these differences are most pronounced concerns the extent of judicial control over the treatment of banks in distress.[33]

Among the areas of the law that are particularly important for banking activities and therefore deserve special attention are the following:

- Central bank law and banking law, as well as payment systems law, are essential to establish adequate institutional and legal frameworks for domestic monetary and financial systems, including, in particular, the prudential regulation of banks.

- Good governance of banks is often addressed in provisions of the banking law that recognize the special status and needs of banks. Thus, for instance, the banking law often includes requirements concerning the corporate form that banks must take and the experience and other qualifications of bank managers. Logically, these provisions should not extend beyond what is necessary to serve the systemic interests by which they are inspired. What this means in practice depends largely on the traditions of each country and its experience with systemic banking problems.

- The law of property and the law of contract govern most aspects of banking activities. Although most countries have an adequate system of contract law, some emerging market economies and especially countries in transition to a market economy have inadequate systems of property law. For banks, such inadequacies are particularly troublesome in activities involving book-entry securities or collateral property.

- The law of negotiable instruments and letters of credit is of special importance to banks, as they are at the heart of most banking activities in international trade. The instruments include in particular bills

---

[33] See Chapter VIII, Section 4, below.

of lading,[34] bills of exchange, and promissory notes. Because bills of lading serve as documents of title to the goods specified on them, they are often used to secure obligations to pay for the goods. In many countries, the domestic law of negotiable instruments is dominated by uniform law established by international conventions.

- Securities law, both commercial and regulatory, is required to govern securities and related financial products, as well as their transfer, public issue, and trading, to regulate the exchanges where securities are listed, and to provide oversight of broker-dealers and other members of the securities industry. The expanding use by banks of publicly traded securities and financial derivatives, *inter alia*, to meet their funding needs, to market their loan assets, and to hedge financial risks, and the constant development of novel securities' products, requires frequent adaptations in this part of the law, often to "codify" internationally established contract practices.

- The law of secured transactions is indispensable for an efficient financial sector. The perfection of mortgages, liens, and other collateral rights requires title registers for real estate and various categories of movable property (cars, trucks, ships, and airplanes) and an extensive administration system.

- The law of enforcement of financial claims is of key importance for banks. Although, quite appropriately, much attention has been devoted to adequate insolvency procedures, many insolvencies, including bank insolvencies, can be avoided if the legal framework supports creditors in the enforcement of their money claims with proper procedures for conservatory attachment of, and execution of judgments against, assets of the debtor. Fast-track judicial proceedings should be available for collection on negotiable instruments, such as bills of exchange and promissory notes.

- Bank insolvency law providing for a regulatory bank administration regime in the banking law or making general insolvency law applicable to banks is an essential component of an effective system of financial law.

A legal system is an organism whose parts are interrelated and dependent on each other. Therefore, reform of part of a legal system cannot

---

[34] Under common law, a bill of lading is not a true negotiable instrument. E.g., in the *United States*, the Uniform Commercial Code restricts the use of the term "negotiable instrument" to orders and promises of payment of money; U.C.C. § 3-104(a). In common law, a bill of lading must be made negotiable by its terms—and it usually is—by providing that delivery of the goods is to the order of the consignee named in the bill.

be productive without covering the other interrelated parts. Generally, to be successful, legal system reform must follow a holistic approach.

To be effective in a democratic society, law must be largely accepted and complied with by the people on a voluntary basis. Just as bank regulation cannot succeed without voluntary compliance by the banks, so a legal system cannot succeed without voluntary respect for and compliance with the rule of law by the population as a whole.

It is difficult to establish such respect and compliance in societies where they are wanting; often, this will require major social changes that take considerable time to develop. This is confirmed by experience in societies emerging from a repressive dictatorship or from chaos, where law reform fails to take root until a minimum of social cohesion, based on morality or enlightened self-interest, begins to foster voluntary compliance with the rule of law for the sake of an emerging democratic socioeconomic order. This process may be accelerated somewhat by appropriate economic incentives and disincentives, by ensuring that law reform reflects social reality, by making the people stake holders in compliance with the law, and by offering alternative procedures and institutions for dispute resolution based on commercial arbitration.

Especially, to promote voluntary compliance, the law must be rooted in the law-consciousness of the people. In particular, law reform should not outpace social growth; where it does, it is often ineffective and its nonenforcement tends to reinforce disrespect for the rule of law. In essence, law must be grown at home, even though importing foreign legislation may have some success in technical areas of the law. And, foreign law so imported must take root to be fruitful. All this takes time. In some countries, the completion of law reform may take several generations.

2. International Aspects

With the expansion of international financial markets, banks increasingly become parties to transactions governed by unfamiliar foreign law. Considerable progress has been made in reducing differences between national legal systems by harmonizing commercial law through international conventions, especially in international sales, payments, and payment arrangements, as well as in negotiable instruments, such as bills of exchange, bills of lading, and promissory notes. In addition, international financial transactions benefit from a growing global uniformity of commercial practices and contract documentation.[35]

Notwithstanding these advances, banks are exposed to the risk that, in the event of a contractual default by a foreign party, claims may have to be pursued in foreign jurisdictions. Creditor banks try to avoid this complication by including in their financial contracts covenants permitting them to bring claims before their own courts; however, judgments supporting claims so adjudicated at home must often be executed against assets abroad, requiring cooperation from foreign courts in aid of execution of those judgments in their jurisdictions. A global convention on the recognition and enforcement of foreign money judgments is urgently needed to support the growing volume and importance of international financial transactions.

3. General Protection for Banks: Principles of Administrative Law

In most democratic market-based societies, the state is the servant of the people. From this principle, administrative law has distilled the rule that individual rights may be restricted by the state only if such restriction serves a public interest that is so strong as to justify the restriction and if the restriction does not extend beyond what is necessary to serve that public interest. For banks, these individual rights include, in particular, the right to freedom of economic activity. Consequently, for banks in democratic market-based societies, individual freedom of economic decision making is the rule and the licensing or regulation of that freedom by the state is the exception.

In most countries, to be effective, bank regulation by the state or a state agency such as the bank regulator must be authorized by statute. This means that there must be a proper banking law governing the licensing and prudential supervision of banks, establishing a bank regulator, and providing sufficient and clearly defined powers to the bank regulator to do all that is required of him in granting and revoking banking licenses, in issuing and enforcing prudential regulations, and in taking corrective action. It means that, in using its authority, the bank regulator must stay within the scope of the law.

---

[35] Relatively recent examples are the standardized documentation for foreign exchange and derivatives transactions issued by the International Swap and Derivatives Association (ISDA) and the Uniform Customs and Practice for Documentary Credits issued by the International Chamber of Commerce.

Most countries also have a branch of the law called administrative law, which generally regulates state authority in order to protect the rights of the people against the improper exercise of power by the state.[36] Over the years, their courts and legislatures have developed principles and rules of administrative law that set standards of good administration. Thus, administrative law requires the state to exercise only powers granted to it by law and not to abuse or misuse those powers. Administrative law also requires that administrative acts are transparent and impartial, and that they do not result from arbitrary and capricious decision making. For instance, the requirement of transparency is generally understood to mean that regulations must include an introductory explanation of their objectives and the legal authority for their issue, that they are published, that they take effect only after a reasonable notice period following their publication, and that they do not operate retroactively. In addition, the law may prescribe participation of interested parties in regulatory decisions by providing that their comments on draft regulations be solicited or that they be invited to attend regulatory hearings of immediate concern to them. In many countries, the law requires that regulatory decisions are published or otherwise notified to all parties whose interests are directly affected by them. In most countries, bank regulators are regarded as agents of the state that are subject to these principles of administrative law.[37] Regulatory acts constituting an abuse or misuse of authority pursuant to principles of administrative law would be characterized as *ultra vires* rendering the acts ineffective under the law.

Often, the law grants the regulator a degree of discretion in exercising its power so as to permit a flexible response to changing circumstances.[38] In judging what is a proper exercise of discretionary powers by the state, administrative law has developed legal principles to arrive at a proper balance between public and private interests.

Under administrative law, it is generally accepted that prudential regulation curtailing the freedom of economic activity of banks requires careful justification. Less well understood is that the mere fact that a prudential regulation would serve some public interest is not enough to justify that regulation. When a proposed regulation or prudential measure would restrict banking activities, the question is not only whether there are public interests that would be served by such regulation or measure but also

---

[36] This is supported by the fact that in many countries administrative law was born of an arduous and long-lasting struggle to curtail the powers of the sovereign.

[37] See, for *Canada*, Deborah M. Duffy, "Canada," in *International Bank Insolvencies: A Central Bank's Perspective,*" ed. by Mario Giovanoli and Gregor Heinrich (The Hague: Kluwer Law International), 1999, at p. 44.

[38] See Chapter III, Section 2, below, for a discussion of discretion of the bank regulator.

and especially whether those interests are so strong and compelling that they outweigh the right to freedom of economic activity that the regulation or measure would restrict. The greater the restriction is expected to be, the stronger the interests served by the prudential regulation or measure should be. For banking regulation this means that, if society attaches great weight to the freedom of economic activity of banks, any restriction of that freedom will require a justification with an even greater counterweight. These considerations apply in particular to determining the limits of regulatory power to intervene in the affairs of banks in distress, because there state intervention is often at its most forceful and intrusive.

Also, in many countries, administrative law requires that restrictions on individual rights do not extend beyond what is necessary to serve the public interest by which they are justified.[39] For instance, a bank in distress should not be closed on the ground of insignificant infractions of financial requirements that do not threaten the bank's liquidity or solvency or the banking system. In some countries this concept is known as "the principle of proportionality";[40] in other countries, the principle of proportionality may be implicitly included under broader norms of administrative law, such as the principle of reasonableness or the prohibition of abuse of discretionary power.[41]

An example of the application of the principle of proportionality to banks (and other financial institutions) is found in *England* in the

---

[39] For example, the police should not use more force than is strictly necessary to maintain public order or to arrest a person.

[40] The principle of proportionality is well known in Europe: Article 73(2) of the Treaty of the European Community of Coal and Steel; *European Court of Justice*: decisions of November 29, 1956, case 8/55 (Fedechar), and July 14, 1972, case 48/69 (I.C.I.); *England*: Section 2(3)(c) of the Financial Services and Markets Act 2000 and H.W.R. Wade, *Administrative Law*, fifth edition, Chapter 12; *Netherlands*: van Wijk en Konijnenbelt, *Hoofdstukken van Administratief Recht*, 1997, at 7:56.The principle of proportionality is also known in international law. See Art.29(2) of the United Nations Universal Declaration of Human Rights of 1948, providing that " *[I]n the exercise of his rights and freedoms, everyone shall be subject only to such limitations as are determined by law solely for the purpose of . . . meeting the just requirements of morality, public order and the general welfare in a democratic society.*" See also the phrase used in Articles 12(3), 18(3), 21 and 22(2) of the International Covenant on Civil and Political Rights of 1966 (999 UNTS 171), that the rights addressed by the provisions *"shall not be subject to any restrictions except those that . . . are necessary to protect . . .* (national security, public order, public health or morals) . . .".

[41] *United States*: K.C. Davis, *Administrative Law Treatise*, second edition, at 29:1–7. The prohibition of abuse of discretionary power implies the existence of a variable normative base line from which abuse is measured: what may constitute abuse of regulatory discretion in trivial circumstances may be reasonable in serious circumstances. The principle of proportionality requires that there be a reasonable relationship between the seriousness of the circumstances at issue and the severity of the regulatory response that these circumstances evoke.

before-mentioned principle of good regulation requiring the Financial Services Authority in discharging its general functions to have regard to:

> the principle that a burden or restriction which is imposed on a person, or on the carrying on of an activity, should be proportionate to the benefits, considered in general terms, which are expected to result from the imposition of that burden or restriction.[42]

The principle of proportionality is not only restrictive but also prescriptive: it not only establishes boundaries to preempt excesses of regulatory authority; it also prohibits regulatory measures that would be too weak to be effective. Thus, the principle of proportionality combats both regulatory abuse and negligent regulatory forbearance.

Owing to the broad and sometimes invasive powers that the law grants to bank regulators, banks are particularly vulnerable to regulatory abuse or misuse of those powers. The broader the grounds on which the law authorizes corrective action against banks, the larger the discretion that the bank regulator may exercise in using such authority, and the greater the role that the administrative law principle of proportionality must play.

Proportionality in bank regulation is required not only on the before-mentioned legal grounds but also because it is sound regulatory practice. Regulatory sanctions that are too severe, if they are published or attract publicity, may adversely affect the bank's reputation and standing in the financial markets that prudential regulation is designed to help maintain. For banks in distress, disproportionate corrective measures could have the unintended effect of depriving the bank of financing on which its rehabilitation depends. Too much prudential medicine can kill the patient.

Because inequality of regulatory treatment is unfair, administrative law incorporates the principle of equality of treatment. In banking regulation, this principle is supported by an important economic consideration—namely, that it is desirable to maintain a level field of competition for all banks in order to avoid economic distortions. As was noted before, if some banks would be subject to a more lenient regulatory regime than others—for instance, because they would be deemed insignificant from a systemic point of view—such banks would enjoy an unfair competitive advantage through a lower regulatory cost base than other banks that would be subject to stricter regulation.

---

[42] Section 2(3)(c) of the Financial Services and Markets Act 2000.

The foregoing applies in particular to the enforcement of exit policies to failing banks. Generally, transparent exit policies are part of every effective system of bank regulation. Apart from the need for equality of treatment for reasons of equity, there are sound economic reasons why exit policies should be uniformly, consistently, and rigorously enforced with respect to all banks: their function of penalizing bad banking practices and thereby discouraging excessive risk taking on the part of banks would be undermined if some banks would be exempted from these policies, creating a moral hazard. There are therefore good reasons for letting all failing banks fail alike.

Nevertheless, in banking regulation bank regulators and monetary authorities tend to make exceptions to the principle of equality of treatment in order to preserve some banks in distress (while permitting other banks to fail), when this is deemed necessary for the protection and continued operation of the banking system as a whole. A mindless application of the principle of equality of treatment could ultimately lead to the closure of the entire banking system. As such a catastrophic event must be avoided, exceptions must be made. Banks whose failure would inflict intolerable harm on the banking system will be saved or merged with another financial institution, while systemically insignificant banks will be permitted to perish. As a consequence, bank regulators also tend to devote greater preventive attention and resources to banks that are deemed "too big to fail" than to other banks. Of course, bank regulators will avoid *a priori* decisions about which banks are and which banks are not to be saved, so as to reduce the risk of moral hazard.

How, in practice, the need to protect the banking system from collapse is to be reconciled with the need to ensure equality of regulatory treatment belongs to the art of bank regulation. In any event, no bank may expect to receive exceptional regulatory treatment without systemic reasons that outweigh the need for equality. Generally speaking, the more regulatory action is confined to enforcement action the more weight will be accorded to the principle of equality of treatment; as regulatory action moves from enforcement into corrective action, the weight will shift toward systemic considerations so as to permit the rescue or sale of systemically significant banks.

Bank regulators and their staff will usually follow internal rules and procedures for their regulatory activities that are designed to maintain compliance with the principles of administrative law. However, compliance with administrative law may be problematic for outside experts employed by the bank regulator for special tasks. This may be the case for former bank managers and even for licensed insolvency practitioners employed by the bank regulator as provisional administrators or receivers of banks. Often, such experts are unfamiliar with administrative law and conduct their activities outside the immediate control and supervision of the regulator. Therefore, when they exercise powers that derive from the bank regulator, compliance with administrative law is not always ensured. This argues for restricting the powers of such agents to the powers of the bank's owners and the bank's management that they replace. If the exercise of regulatory powers exceeding those of owners and managers is deemed indispensable, it should be accompanied by procedural safeguards ensuring respect for principles of administrative law—for instance, by submitting decisions of a regulatory nature to the prior consent of the regulator.

4. Special Protection for Banks: Provisions of Banking Law

A comparison at the national level of the authority granted by the law to various agencies of the state shows that, in most countries, the powers of the bank regulator go significantly beyond those granted to other public agencies. These greater powers of the bank regulator are justified because they are needed to serve the public interest in a safe and sound banking system. They come at a cost, however: banks are subject to more regulatory interference in their affairs than other types of enterprise.

This does not mean that the authority of the bank regulator would be unfettered. In general, the powers of the bank regulator are restricted in scope by rules of administrative law and by the provisions of banking law granting those powers. These restrictions may take the form of procedures providing for an administrative or judicial review of regulatory decisions and actions at the request of interested parties, subject to the need to exempt from such review emergency intervention when urgently needed. Ultimately, the bank regulator may be condemned to pay damages caused by an unlawful exercise of its powers.

However, general principles of administrative law do not afford greater protection to banks than to others. As the restrictions they impose on regulatory authority are by and large the same for all regulators, they do not neutralize the heavier regulatory burden carried by the banking industry. And banking law, instead of increasing the protection afforded by review procedures in order to compensate for more intrusive banking regulation, often does the opposite by curtailing the use of review procedures for situations that present significant systemic threats and require immediate corrective action lest they spin out of control. The argument is that nature and risks of banking do not always allow time for the deliberate and adversarial decision making and review procedures that generally mark other types of regulation.

This double burden imposed on banks is not inconsistent with administrative law. As was noted before, the principle of proportionality requires not only that restrictions on individual rights do not extend beyond what is necessary to serve the public interest by which they are justified, but also that restrictions are imposed on individual rights when they are needed to serve the public interest by which they are justified. Applied to banking regulation, this generally means that a greater threat posed to the public by banking activities must be met by more intrusive regulation with less protection for the interests of banks.

In different societies the competing interests of the banks and the public are assigned different weights, and consequently, the banking laws of the countries reviewed differ in the protection they afford to interests of banks. The balance between the public interest in swift and effective regulatory action and the interests of banks seems to be largely determined by the legal traditions of each country. In countries whose sociopolitical framework leans toward a command culture, the banking law will tend to grant more freedom of action to the regulator and proportionately less protection to the banks than in countries whose societies prize a consensual approach to decision making.

Several techniques are used in banking laws for calibrating this balance. First and foremost, the powers of the bank regulator should be carefully defined in the law so as to delineate the boundaries of regulatory discretion. Sloppy statutory language as to the authority of the bank regulator creates uncertainty and tends to increase banking transaction costs. Although, ultimately, the boundaries of regulatory authority and the corresponding rights of banks may find *ex post* clarification in the courts, it is vastly preferable if they are defined *ex ante* by the law. Moreover, and generally speaking, legal certainty is better served by clear statutory language than by case law born of the idiosyncrasies of fact-oriented judicial decisions.

As stated before, the banking law may protect the interests of banks and their owners by imposing special notice and hearing requirements on bank regulators.[43] For example, in *Canada*, the law prescribes that, before the bank regulator may take control of a bank or its assets, the bank must be given notice of the action proposed to be taken and of the bank's right to make written representations to the regulator within the time specified in the notice, not exceeding ten days after it receives the notice.[44] Exceptionally, the law provides procedural protection to banks by providing that, when taking certain measures, the bank regulator functions as an administrative judicial authority.[45]

There are matters, however, that do not tolerate the delays inherent in hearings. Some matters are so urgent or serious that they require immediate corrective action on the part of the regulator. Other matters, such as the appointment of a provisional administrator or conservator, may require secrecy, especially if bank owners or managers cannot be trusted. And, where the language of the law is mandatory and requires the regulator to intervene, there is no need to give prior notice of the regulator's intentions to the bank.[46] For such cases, the banking law may exempt the regulator from notice or hearing requirements.[47] However, the principle of proportionality demands that such exemptions apply only in the conditions by which they are justified: for instance, and apart from legal principle, the logic is inescapable that the authority of the bank regulator to take swift action without prior hearing in cases of urgency should be limited to cases of urgency.

In *England*, the banking law provides that the bank regulator need not notify a bank of its intentions in respect of the imposition or variation of a restriction on a banking license in any case in which the bank regulator considers that the restriction should be imposed or var-

---

[43] *Canada*: Section 645(2) of the Bank Act; *England*: Section 13 of the Banking Act 1987; *France*: Article 42 of Law No. 84-46 on the Activities and Supervision of Credit Institutions; *Spain*: Article 33 of Law No. 22/1988 on Supervision and Intervention with respect to Credit Institutions; *United States*: 12 U.S.C. § 1818(b)(1).

[44] Section 648(1.2) of the Bank Act; *cf.* Section 39.1 of the Canada Deposit Insurance Corporation Act for similar requirements when a procedure is begun to vest the shares of the bank in the CDIC or to appoint the CDIC as receiver of the bank.

[45] In *France*, the Banking Commission is regarded as an administrative court when it takes decisions to impose certain disciplinary sanctions; see Article 48(1) of Law No. 84-46 on the Activities and Supervision of Credit Institutions.

[46] *England*: Section 14(1) of the Banking Act 1987.

[47] See, e.g., *France*: Article 48(2) of Law No. 84-46 on the Activities and Supervision of Credit Institutions; *Spain*: Article 33 of Law No. 22/1988 on Supervision and Intervention with respect to Credit Institutions, providing that no hearing is required if it would cause delays that would severely prejudice the effectiveness of the action taken or the economic interests at stake.

ied "as a matter of urgency." In any such case the regulator may by written notice to the bank impose or vary the restriction, stating the reasons for the action. Thereupon, the bank has fourteen days in which to make representations to the regulator. Within twenty-eight days from when the notice was given, the regulator, taking into account any representations made by the bank, must decide whether to confirm or rescind its original decision or whether to impose a different restriction or to vary the restriction in a different manner, and must give the bank written notice thereof, stating the reasons for the decision unless the original decision is rescinded. This notice takes effect from the date on which it is given.[48]

The criterion of urgency is not the only standard used to exempt regulatory intervention from notice or hearing requirements.

The banking law of *Canada* provides that no cease or desist direction shall be issued to a bank unless the bank is provided with a reasonable opportunity to make representations in the matter, but that, where, in the opinion of the bank regulator, the length of time required for such representations might be "prejudicial to the public interest," the regulator may make a temporary direction with respect to those matters having effect for a period of not more than fifteen days.[49]

In the *United States*, the law specifies extensive notice and hearing procedures for the issue of a cease and desist order by the regulator to a bank in response to an unsafe or unsound practice in conducting the bank's business or a violation of a law, rule, or regulation or a condition imposed by the regulator. The procedure begins with the service of a notice of charges upon the bank, stating the pertinent facts and fixing the time and place for a hearing to determine whether a cease and desist order should issue against the bank. The hearing must take place neither earlier than 30 days nor later than 60 days after service of the notice unless an earlier date is set by the regulator at the bank's request. If upon the record made at the hearing the regulator finds that any violation or unsafe or unsound practice specified in the notice of charges has been established, the regulator may issue a cease and desist order. Normally, the order becomes effective at the expiration of thirty days after the service of the order upon the bank.[50]

However, if the regulator determines that the violation or unsafe or unsound practice specified in the notice of charges is "likely to cause

---

[48] Section 14 of the Banking Act 1987.
[49] Section 645(2) and (3) of the Bank Act.
[50] 12 U.S.C. § 1818(b).

insolvency or significant dissipation of assets or earnings of the bank, or is likely to weaken the condition of the bank or otherwise prejudice the interests of its depositors prior to the completion of the administrative proceedings conducted pursuant to the notice of charges," the regulator may issue a temporary cease and desist order that becomes effective upon service on the bank and, unless set aside, limited, or suspended by a court, remains effective and enforceable pending the completion of the administrative proceedings pursuant to the notice and until the charges are dismissed or until the effective date of a cease and desist order issued pursuant to such proceedings.[51]

In several countries, the law follows a two-step approach consisting of orders given to a bank to correct a problem, followed by more stringent corrective action if the bank fails to comply.[52] Affording a bank a reasonable opportunity to solve its problems on its own accord, and allowing it time to consult thereon with the bank regulator before corrective measures are imposed by the regulator, is an appropriate procedure for safeguarding the bank's interests.

The foregoing points to the conclusion that some countries use a graduated approach toward the protection of banks and their owners under the banking law: the more intrusive regulatory intervention is, the more protection should be afforded against regulatory abuse. Sometimes, however, this trend runs in the other direction: in the *United States*, while for cease and desist orders the interests of banks are generally protected by the before-mentioned requirements of advance notices and hearings, the bank regulator may impose the much more invasive measure of appointing a conservator or a receiver for a bank without prior notice or hearing.[53]

Perhaps the most successful technique used in banking law to protect the interests of banks and their owners is to make them stake-

---

[51] 12 U.S.C. § 1818(c)(1). Within ten days after service of the temporary order, the bank may apply to the court for an injunction setting aside, limiting, or suspending the enforcement, operation, or effectiveness of the temporary order pending the completion of the administrative proceedings pursuant to the notice of charges: 12 U.S.C. § 1818(c)(2).

[52] *Belgium*: Article 57(1) of the Law on the Statute and Supervision of Credit Institutions; *Canada*: Sections 485(3)(a) *juncto* 648(1.1) of the Bank Act; *France*: Articles 43 *juncto* 45 of Law No. 84-46 on the Activities and Supervision of Credit Institutions; *Germany*: Section 45(2) of the Law on the Credit System; *Luxembourg*: Article 59(1) and (2) of the Law of 1993 on the Financial Sector; *Netherlands*: Article 28(2) and (3) of the Law on Supervision of the Credit System.

[53] Compare 12 U.S.C. § 1818(b) for cease and desist orders with 12 U.S.C. § 191 for the appointment of a receiver and 12 U.S.C. § 203 for the appointment of a conservator.

holders in corrective action through their agreement to a corrective action plan.[54] These plans are discussed more fully below.[55]

5. Review of Regulatory Acts

Regulatory acts are reviewed either before they are done (*ex ante* review) or after they are done (*ex post* review).

Ex Ante Review of Regulatory Acts[56]

In several countries, the law submits certain categories of regulatory decisions whose effects on banks are particularly invasive to the *ex ante* review of a higher administrative authority or the courts for authorizing or taking the proposed decision. Examples are found in the appointment of provisional administrators and receivers in order to take control of a bank.[57] As is discussed in greater detail below, the need to protect interested parties is an important argument for submitting the receivership of banks to a court-supervised procedure instead of a regulatory procedure without judicial oversight.[58]

Countries differ in their judgment as to what rises to the level where *ex ante* judicial intervention is required. For instance, in some countries, the voting rights of bank shareholders may be suspended only by court order,[59] while in other countries this is left to the bank regulator.[60]

Ex ante review procedures serve a dual purpose. They serve not only the interests of the banks, but also the interests of the bank regulator

---

[54] *Argentina*: Article 34 of the Financial Institutions Law; *Portugal*: Article 141 sub(a) of the Legal Framework of Credit Institutions and Financial Companies, approved by Decree-Law No. 298/92; *Japan*: Article 26(1) of the Banking Law; *United States*: 12 U.S.C. § 1831o(e)(2).

[55] See Chapter IV, Section 3, below.

[56] The *ex ante* review addressed here requiring the prior approval of regulatory acts by a higher administrative authority or the judiciary should be distinguished from the *ex post* review of regulatory acts discussed below.

[57] See Chapter IX, Section 2, and Chapter X, Section 2, below.

[58] See Chapter VIII, Section 4, below.

[59] *Austria*: Article 20(6)3 of the Austrian Banking Act; *France*: Article 46-1 of Law No. 84-46 on the Activities and Supervision of Credit Institutions.

[60] *Germany*: Section 46(1) of the Law on the Credit System; *Italy*: 70(2) of the Law of 1993 on Matters Concerning Banking and Credit, albeit as an effect of provisional administration ordered by the regulator; *Luxembourg*: Article 59(2) of the Law of 1993 on the Financial Sector; *Netherlands*: Article 28(3) of the Law on Supervision of the Credit System.

in that they help ensure that the regulator complies with the rule of law. This enhances public confidence in the bank regulator. In a democratic society, public confidence in the regulator is based on respect for and compliance with the rule of law. Judicial review of regulatory acts, whether in the first instance or on appeal, is a valuable instrument for confirming to the public that the regulator respects the rule of law. Moreover, where compliance with the rule of law on the part of the bank regulator is deficient, voluntary compliance with prudential law on the part of the banking industry will be wanting.

Ex Post Review of Regulatory Acts

For similar reasons, banks should be afforded a reasonable opportunity to complain *ex post* of alleged abuse or misuse of regulatory power before impartial and qualified administrative tribunals or ad hoc review panels. And, where bank regulatory acts are submitted to an *ex ante* administrative or judicial review by an authority other than the bank regulator, the law should offer judicial appeal. Accordingly, and apart from the possibility to sue for damages in civil court, many national laws provide for some form of *ex post* administrative or judicial review and revision of administrative decisions and other acts.

Review of the acts of the bank regulator may be either administrative or judicial. Administrative review may be performed by a higher organ of the decision-making agency or by a higher administrative authority. Judicial review may be performed either by administrative courts or tribunals, or by the civil courts.

The review of regulatory acts may concern a review of the legality of the acts or a review of their merits. In this brief discussion, a review of the legality of regulatory acts will be understood to cover only legality in a strict sense—namely, the questions whether the acts were authorized by law, and whether they comply with statutory requirements or violate boundaries set by the law to the discretion of regulators; a review as to the merits will be taken to mean a *de novo* review of all aspects of regulatory acts, including not only whether the acts are appropriate from a strict legal viewpoint but also whether they are appropriate from a standpoint of public administration. Whereas a review of the legality of an act applies only legal arguments, a review of the merits of an act also includes other considerations, such as economic and political arguments.

A review of the legality of regulatory acts will normally involve a review of the acts in light of the statutory authority for the acts, their compliance with procedural and substantive requirements specified by law, and their consistency with legal standards of good administration such as proportionality and equality of treatment.

Whereas the review of administrative acts as to their legality is not problematic in principle, the broader review of administrative acts as to their merits is, insofar as it requires the reviewing authority to take the seat of the regulator and to examine the decision under review *de novo*. To be done properly, a review of the merits of an act requires a degree of expertise that is at least equal to that of the agency that acted.

Therefore, a review of the merits of a regulatory act is generally carried out only by a higher organ of the decision-making agency or by a higher administrative authority or by an administrative court or tribunal, and not by the civil courts. Civil courts are often reluctant to extend their review beyond the legality of a regulatory act to its merits, not only because they would lack the necessary expertise to consider nonlegal aspects but sometimes also for reasons related to the constitutional separation between the judiciary and the executive branches of state, particularly where the law grants or leaves the regulator a measure of discretion.[61]

In civil court, the review of a regulatory act will often identify a certain area of discretion of the regulator, an area of decision making where the law grants the regulator autonomy of judgment. In this area of regulatory autonomy, the civil court will generally refrain from substituting its own judgment for that of the regulator and limit its review to the strictly legal question whether the regulatory act respects the boundaries of the law. Thus, for instance, in applying the principle of proportionality to a regulatory decision, the civil court would not determine what in its judgment would have been a proportional response to the circumstances underlying the decision—reasonable men can differ as to what is proportional—but it would restrict its review to the question whether the response was clearly disproportional to the circumstances. In this sense, the judicial review of regulatory discretion is usually a *marginal* review that considers only regulatory violations of the boundaries set by the law to administrative discretion. Accordingly, and in contrast with the standards of good administration, which generally are expressed in positive terms, the standards applied by the civil courts in their review of regulatory discretion are often expressed in negative terms, as evidenced by the fol-

---

[61] See Chapter III, Section 2, below, for a brief discussion of discretion of the bank regulator.

lowing words and clauses: *discriminatory, excessive, arbitrary and capricious, abuse of discretion,* and *clearly erroneous.*

It is widely accepted that, in principle, measures taken by the bank regulator should be subject to review by a higher administrative authority or by the administrative or civil courts. Article 6 of the European Convention on Human Rights provides that, in the determination of his civil rights and obligations, everyone is entitled to a fair and public hearing within a reasonable time by an independent and impartial tribunal established by law. Accordingly, Article 13 of the First European Banking Directive provides that member states shall ensure that decisions taken in respect of a credit institution in pursuance to laws, regulations, and administrative provisions adopted in accordance with the Directive may be subject to the right to apply to the courts, and that the same shall apply where no decision is taken within six months of its submission in respect of an application for authorization that contains all the information required under the provisions in force.

However, it is equally generally accepted that the bank regulator must have the power to act swiftly and decisively in taking the corrective measures required to protect the banking system or the interests of depositors and other creditors from the consequences of the failure of a bank to comply with prudential standards. The possibility of review of regulatory measures taken by the bank regulator raises difficult questions of balance between these competing interests.

Lest appeals of regulatory decisions would delay urgent regulatory action, the law of some countries provides that decisions of the bank regulator ordering corrective measures or a takeover of a bank are enforceable immediately, notwithstanding their appeal,[62] although interested parties may be able to obtain a court order or a decision of the regulator suspending enforcement. In other countries, however, regulatory decisions are suspended pending their appeal, except for decisions that specifically provide otherwise.[63]

In some countries, appeals from regulatory decisions are brought before the civil courts. For instance, in the *United States*, a bank may

---

[62] *Germany*: Section 49 of the Law on the Credit System; *Luxembourg*: Article 60(9) of the Law on the Financial Sector. In *England*, Section 27(5) of the Banking Act 1987 provides that the Banking Appeal Tribunal may suspend the operation of the decision under appeal, implying that otherwise the decision remains in effect pending appeal.

[63] *Belgium*: Article 57(2) of the Law on the Statute and Supervision of Credit Institutions.

obtain a review of an order served by the bank regulator to cease and desist from an unsafe or unsound practice or violation of law, by filing a petition in a federal court of appeals.[64]

In other countries, the law may provide for administrative review of regulatory decisions on appeal, either before the general administrative courts or before a special tribunal. Examples are found in *the Netherlands* where decisions of the bank regulator are subject to review by the administrative courts under the General Administrative Law Act, while the banking law provides also for a special appeal to the Appeals Board for Trade and Industry;[65] in *Denmark* where decisions of the bank regulator are subject to review by a more or less independent Companies Appeals Board established by the Ministry of Industry;[66] and in *England* where appeals can be brought before the Banking Appeal Tribunal.[67] In *Belgium*[68] and *Spain*,[69] the Minister of Finance is the authority to review decisions of the bank regulator; while in *Italy*,[70] jurisdiction for review of decisions of the bank regulator is given to the Interministerial Committee of Credit and Savings, consisting of several cabinet members, including the Minister of the Treasury as chairman. Where these authorities are not politically independent, the risk of partiality exists. Yet, that risk is inherent in most administrative review at higher levels of government. In any event, the quasi-judicial tribunals listed might not qualify as courts under Article 13 of the First European Banking Directive or as independent and impartial tribunals under Article 6 of the European Convention on Human Rights.

In *England*, reviews of decisions of the bank regulator are heard by a specially constituted ad hoc administrative tribunal, the Banking Appeal Tribunal.[71] Whenever a request for a review is lodged with the secretary of the Tribunal, the Lord Chancellor and the Chancellor of the Exchequer must appoint the three members of the Tribunal who are to carry out the review. The composition of the Tribunal—an expe-

---

[64] 12 U.S.C. § 1818(h)(2).

[65] Article 90 of the Law on Supervision of Credit Institutions.

[66] Article 52b of the Consolidated Banking Law.

[67] Section 27 of the Banking Act 1987; see below for a discussion.

[68] Article 57(2) of the Law on the Statute and Supervision of Credit Institutions.

[69] Article 2 of the Law 13/1994 (as amended) on the Autonomy of the Banco de España.

[70] Article 9 of the Law of 1993 on Matters Concerning Banking and Credit.

[71] Section 28 of the Banking Act 1987, and the Banking Appeal Tribunal Regulations issued pursuant to the Banking Act. *Cf.*, Part IX of, and Schedule 13 to, the Financial Services and Markets Act 2000 for the Financial Services and Markets Tribunal, with similar jurisdiction.

rienced lawyer appointed by the Lord Chancellor as chairman and two members, one an accountant and one a banker—is designed to ensure a professional judgment. The proceedings of the Tribunal are held *in camera* so as to preserve confidentiality and to help avoid leaks of sensitive information to the financial markets. The review by the Banking Appeal Tribunal is limited by law to the determination of the question: ... "whether, for the reasons adduced by the appellant, the decision was unlawful or not justified by the evidence on which it was based."[72] The Tribunal may confirm or reverse the decision of the bank regulator but it does not have the power to vary the decision; it may, however, in certain cases, direct the regulator to vary its decision subject to the power of the regulator to decide how its decision should be varied.[73] Both parties may appeal the decision of the Tribunal to the High Court; if the High Court is of the opinion that the decision of the Tribunal was "erroneous in point of law" it must remit the matter to the Tribunal for re-hearing and determination by it;[74] thereby, the law limits the scope of review by the civil courts of Tribunal decisions on appeal quite properly to questions of legality and excludes that the courts would submit Tribunal decisions on appeal to a review on the merits.[75]

The English Banking Appeal Tribunal may serve as a model for other countries, and not only because it meets the criteria of the First European Banking Directive and the European Convention on Human Rights. By its limited scope of review and by bringing a measure of independence and professional expertise to the review process, the tribunal provides safeguards that are missing from review proceedings in other countries. In view of the seriousness of banking regulation, the question must be whether administrative review of decisions of the bank regulator is at all justified in the absence of such safeguards.

---

[72] Section 29 (1) of the Banking Act 1987. *Cf.,* in contrast, Section 133(4) of the Financial Services and Markets Act 2000, which requires the Financial Services and Markets Tribunal to determine *what (if any) is the appropriate action for the Financial Services Authority to take in relation to the matter referred to it.*

[73] Section 29 (2) and (3) of the Banking Act 1987.

[74] Section 31(1) of the Banking Act 1987; subsection (3) excludes further appeal to the Court of Appeal except with the leave of that Court or of the court or judge from whose decision the appeal is brought.

[75] In contrast, Section 137 of the Financial Services and Markets Act 2000 permits the civil courts on appeal to give a decision on the merits: if the court considers that a decision of the Financial Services and Markets Tribunal was wrong in law, it may not only remit the matter to the Tribunal for rehearing and determination but also *itself make a determination.*

Unlike most law governing the review of regulatory acts in the civil courts, the banking law providing for the administrative review of bank regulatory acts often mandates a review on the merits. In banking matters, the authority carrying out the review takes the seat of the bank regulator and must therefore have qualifications worthy of his task. Because of the often highly technical nature of bank regulatory decisions, it cannot be readily assumed that a review panel that is not composed of banking experts—like those serving on an English Banking Appeal Tribunal—will be able to review decisions of the bank regulator with the degree of expertise that such decisions demand.

If the review of bank regulatory decisions must be obtained from a general administrative court instead, it would be appropriate to establish a special division of the court that is qualified to hear banking cases or, alternatively, to require the court to seek advice from one or more independent experts in the field of banking and accountancy and to base its decision on such advice, unless the advice is patently wrong.

To be fair, the review of regulatory acts must be impartial. An essential condition for impartiality is the autonomy of the authority doing the review. This means not only that the authority is functionally and financially independent from the bank regulator in a formal sense but also that the authority is publicly perceived as autonomous and unbiased. The features that help build such perception are generally the same as those of any independent judiciary. In this respect, an administrative court established by law and staffed with judges whose autonomy is ensured by the law has distinct advantages over *ad hoc* tribunals, especially if their judges are appointed or selected by government officials who may have a political interest in the decision of a particular dispute. However, administrative law courts are sometimes seen as having a pro-government bias; this may require the establishment of permanent review panels enjoying a greater aura of impartiality, possibly with representation of the banking industry. Of course, in building a reputation of impartiality, much will depend on the record of the review authority itself.

In practice, it is difficult for a bank to appeal a decision of its regulator, even under the best of circumstances. The extensive powers of bank regulators make them formidable adversaries and allow them to make life difficult and therefore costly for any bank that dares to question their judgment. It is precisely to protect banks from abuse by the regulator in wielding these powers that the law should give them access to an independent and expert review of regulatory decisions, even though in reality this right would be rarely exercised.

However, there are two important considerations that balance the argument for offering banks and their owners an administrative or judicial review of acts of the bank regulator.

The first consideration is that the right to review should not be abused to frustrate proper regulatory intervention. This is particularly important where it concerns regulatory action whose suspension or repeal would be damaging to the banking system, and hence would undermine the authority and credibility of the bank regulator and diminish confidence in the banking system. Some protection against undesirable effects of appeals could be granted by stipulating in the law that some critical decisions are enforceable pending appeal.[76] Or, the law may mandate specific regulatory action in certain narrowly defined circumstances, leaving no room for regulatory discretion and little room for appeal.[77] Alternatively, there are countries where appeals against certain regulatory measures are simply excluded by law;[78] there is a risk, however, that the legality of such exclusions would successfully be challenged on constitutional grounds or pursuant to provisions of international human rights agreements.[79]

The second consideration is that the bank regulator and its staff must be protected against frivolous damage claims brought by bank owners and managers and other interested parties in the civil courts. This need is expressed in the first of the Basle Core Principles, which argues for "[A] suitable legal framework for banking supervision ... including ... legal protection for supervisors."[80] A distinction must be drawn between, on the one hand, suits brought against the bank reg-

---

[76] E.g., *Luxembourg*: Article 60(9) of the Law of 1993 on the Financial Sector.

[77] E.g., *England*: Section 11(6) of the Banking Act 1987, providing that the banking license of a bank must be revoked if a winding up order has been made against it in the United Kingdom, or a resolution for its voluntary winding up in the United Kingdom has been passed.

[78] E.g., *Canada*: Section 39.13(6) of the Canada Deposit Insurance Corporation Act, which excludes any court review of vesting and receivership orders made by the Governor in Council; *Germany*: Section 46b of the Law on the Credit System, which excludes appeal against court decisions opening insolvency proceedings against a bank.

[79] E.g., Article 6 of the European Convention on Human Rights, and accordingly Article 13 of the First European Banking Directive.

[80] See also Section 2.3.3 of the Report of the G-22 Working Group on Strengthening Financial Systems. Protection for regulators from suit should not cover acts that are patently illegal or characterized as gross negligence or willful misconduct. See also René Smits and Ron Luberti, "Supervisory Liability: An Introduction to Several Legal Systems and a Case Study" in *International Bank Insolvencies: A Central Bank's Perspective*," ed. by Mario Giovanoli and Gregor Heinrich (The Hague: Kluwer Law International), 1999.

ulating agency (or the state if the agency has no legal personality), including its staff in their official capacity, and, on the other hand, claims brought against individual members of the agency's staff on a personal basis on account of their official acts or omissions. Claims of the second category should be ruled out by the law, except perhaps in cases of willful personal misconduct not ordered by a superior officer of the agency.

In many countries, the bank regulator enjoys a measure of immunity from suit. Such immunity is bolstered if the law provides for review procedures administered by experts and designed to provide relief to injured parties while protecting the regulator from unreasonable claims. In determining the scope of the immunity of the bank regulator, special consideration should be given to the need to provide a suitable deterrent against gross negligence and willful abuse of power on the part of the bank regulator or its staff.

Although there are good reasons why the law should discourage frivolous claims for damages resulting from regulatory action, there are equally good reasons why the law should support justified tort claims against the bank regulating agency. Regulators are only human, even bank regulators, and mistakes are made. However, these should not be at the risk or for the expense of the bank. The improper character of unlawful activity by the state or its agents can and should be cured by prompt and adequate compensation of damages suffered as a result of such activity, and this not only to establish a more equitable distribution of the costs of regulatory abuse but also to strengthen the justification for permitting urgent regulatory action to proceed pending its review. Thus, for example, in *France*, the state is responsible for deficiencies in prudential supervision by the Banking Commission, which lacks legal personality and capital, but the state is liable for damages only in the relatively rare cases where such deficiencies rise to the level of gross negligence.[81] In countries where the law continues to afford an unreasonable degree of governmental immunity from liability suits, the law should be changed accordingly.[82]

---

[81] Christian Gavalda, and Jean Stoufflet, *Droit Bancaire*, fourth edition, at No. 145.

[82] One of these countries is the *United States*. See for a discussion of U.S. law: Cynthia Crawford Lichtenstein, "Public Liability in U.S. Courts and Brasserie du Pêcheur and Factortane in the European Court" in *Liber Amicorum for Gordon Slynn: Court Review in International Perspective* (The Hague: Kluwer Law International), 2000.

Principal Objectives To Be Pursued by Law

All banks should be submitted to adequate prudential regulation that submits similar banking activities to similar prudential requirements and regulatory costs.

Prudential banking regulation should be assigned to a single financially and operationally autonomous bank regulator, accountable to the public and staffed with sufficient qualified and experienced personnel.

The bank regulator should promote fair competition between banks, foster innovation, and educate the public in financial matters; it should generally constrain the corrective effects of market forces on banks only if required by overriding systemic considerations.

Official liquidity support to banks should be limited in amount and time and should be based on a careful cost-benefit analysis, weighing the cost of moral hazard against the benefit of systemic risk reduction. In the event of a rescue operation, bank owners should be made to pay for the operation's cost. Bank regulators should combat moral hazard that may result from guarantees of official financial assistance to failing banks or their customers, regardless of whether these are implicit or explicit (deposit insurance), by normally permitting bank failures to occur through strict enforcement of explicit exit policies for banks.

In order to help prevent banking problems the law should promote conditions conducive to sound banking systems, including especially an adequate legal framework for banking activities. Countries should accede to the international conventions governing banking activities and should cause their banks to use where possible internationally accepted uniform standards and procedures in their international transactions. A global convention on the recognition and enforcement of foreign money judgments is urgently needed.

Bank regulators and their agents are subject to the rules of administrative law. Prudential law should be written and enforced so that the regulatory measures taken pursuant to the law present a proportional response to the banking deficiencies addressed by the measures. Prudential law should be enforced equally toward all banks, so as to avoid unfair competition between banks. However, in derogation of the principle of equality of regulatory treatment, exceptional regulatory intervention to save some banks while others are permitted to fail may be justified by overriding systemic considerations.

Noncompliance with administrative law by external agents of bank regulators assigned to banks in distress, such as inspectors, provisional administrators, and receivers, may be limited by providing that the powers of inspectors and provisional administrators shall not exceed those of bank managers, and by submitting important decisions of receivers to an ex ante review by the regulator or the court under whose authority they operate.

The law should provide banks, and their owners and creditors, protection from regulatory abuse by affording them a reasonable opportunity to make representations before a regulatory decision affecting their rights is taken, subject to the need for immediate regulatory action if urgently required by overriding interests.

Interested parties should be afforded a reasonable opportunity to have decisions of bank regulators or their agents affecting their rights reviewed by an impartial tribunal, established by or pursuant to law and staffed with judges having sufficient expertise or being assisted by independent experts. As a rule, regulatory decisions under review by a tribunal should remain in effect pending their review, except as the tribunal may otherwise decide.

III

Regulatory Intervention: Common Issues

1. Categories and Objectives of Regulatory Intervention

Regulatory intervention includes all action taken by the bank regulator with respect to a bank in response to continuing violations of prudential law (banking law, implementing regulations, etc.) on the part of that bank. Thereby, the bank regulator intervenes directly or indirectly in the bank's management and operations.

The ultimate objective of regulatory intervention is the same as that of all prudential regulation of banks, namely, to promote an efficient and sound banking system. Its immediate objective is to return a wayward bank to compliance with prudential law or to conserve the value of its assets for its creditors followed by the bank's sale or liquidation.

Regulatory intervention consists of three categories of measures: enforcement action, corrective action, and taking control of a bank through provisional administration or receivership. Distinctions should be drawn between these three levels of regulatory involvement because they differ as to their objectives.

Enforcement of prudential banking law aims at prevention by calling on banks to correct weaknesses before they cause serious banking problems. An example of an enforcement action is a direction or order given by the regulator to a bank engaging in an unsafe or unsound practice in conducting its banking business requiring the bank to cease and desist from the same, without necessarily instructing the bank to take certain specified corrective measures.[83]

---

[83] See, e.g., *France*: Article 43 of Law No. 84-46 on the Activities and Supervision of Credit Institutions; *Germany*: Article 46(1) of the Law on the Credit System; *Netherlands*: Article 28(2) of the Law on Supervision of the Credit System; and *United States*: 12 U.S.C. § 1818(b)(1).

Corrective action is damage repair designed to save the bank and to return it to regulatory health. For example, if it must be feared that a bank, receiving a cease and desist order of the regulator to end an unsafe or unsound banking practice, will fail to take adequate corrective action, the order may prescribe the measures that the bank must take.[84]

In several countries, if the corrective measures ordered are not carried out or fail to have their intended effect or would come too late to be successful, the regulator may take control of the bank and replace the bank's management with one or more provisional administrators whose task is to save the bank by managing it back to compliance with prudential regulations or to prepare the bank for a sale to or merger with another institution. Normally, the corrective treatment of a bank requires the bank's continuing operation. This exposes the creditors of the bank to the risk that, notwithstanding attempts to save the bank, the bank's condition would worsen to a point where the probability of success of continued corrective action becomes too low to justify the risk of further erosion of the value of the bank's assets. As this risk grows, the bank regulator must shift the focus of its objectives to minimizing the systemic effects of the bank's failure and maximizing the value of the bank's assets for its creditors. In such circumstances, when the regulator decides that it is unlikely that the bank can be saved or sold, a receivership may be imposed for closure including liquidation of the bank under receivership. Thus, unsuccessful corrective action tends to resolve itself through bank closure.

For banks in distress, there would ideally be a gradual progression from enforcement of prudential requirements to corrective action that, if unsuccessful, gives way to taking control of the bank through provisional administration or receivership. In reality, however, the various regulatory actions cannot always be taken sequentially and progressively. For instance, the regulator may not have the time to follow a gradual approach and may have to decide on corrective action through a receiver, for instance, to displace crooked owners and directors when bank supervisors uncover serious banking deficiencies that had been fraudulently concealed. The bank regulator must have the freedom to be selective and apply different regulatory measures in response to different banking problems: in extreme cases, this may require an extreme regulatory response.

---

[84] In *United States* practice, cease and desist orders often prescribe long and detailed corrective measures—12 U.S.C. § 1818(b)(1).

2. Discretion of Regulators Under the Law

Most banking laws authorize the bank regulator to order a bank in distress to take corrective measures, or to take control of the bank through provisional administration or a receivership.

As a rule, the scope of the powers of a public agency such as the bank regulator are limited by the statutory provisions (the banking law) granting those powers. Sometimes, the law prescribes more or less precisely when and how a certain authority is to be exercised. More often, however, the law grants the regulator a measure of discretion in deciding when and how a certain power is to be exercised. Discretion in this context means that the decision whether or not to take action and the choice of corrective measures to be imposed on a bank depend to a greater or lesser extent on the judgment of the bank regulator.

In analyzing the law as to the discretion that it grants to the bank regulator, a distinction must be drawn between the legal authority to take regulatory action, the grounds on which that authority may be exercised, and the choice of regulatory action that may be taken pursuant to that authority. This distinction may be illustrated by reference to the following banking law provision:

> When a bank has failed to follow sound banking practices, the bank regulator, after having afforded the bank's managers an opportunity to explain such failure, may issue a warning to them.[85]

In this provision, the legal authority to take corrective action is granted by the provision that the bank regulator may issue a warning. The ground for exercising that authority is that the bank has failed to follow sound banking practices. The choice of action authorized by the law is limited to the issue of a warning to the bank's managers.

Legal Authority to Take Regulatory Action

In the foregoing example, the legal authority to take corrective action is couched in permissive language: the provision says *may* issue a warning. This means that the bank regulator has discretion in deciding whether or not to exercise his authority under the provision. If, in contrast, the provision had used mandatory language and had said

---

[85] *France*: Article 42 of Law No. 84-46 on the Activities and Supervision of Credit Institutions.

shall issue a warning, the regulator would have no discretion in the exercise of his authority: whenever the regulator would determine that a bank had failed to follow sound banking practices, the regulator would be required to take the action prescribed by the law. Of course, even when the provision had used mandatory language, the regulator would have had a fair degree of discretion in determining what are sound banking practices.

The permissive approach raises a serious issue. Assuming that all provisions of the banking law that authorize the bank regulator to take corrective action against a wayward bank are couched in such discretionary language (as is the case in many countries), would then the regulator be permitted not to take any corrective action at all against such bank? As, strictly speaking, the answer must be affirmative, the issue is whether this state of affairs is acceptable. Should the bank regulator not be required by law to address every infraction of the banking law?

Without opening a discussion of regulatory forbearance,[86] the supporters of permissive treatment generally respond that there are circumstances in which discretion is needed. The exercise of remedial authority on the part of the regulator would make little sense, for instance, when the violation at issue is insignificant or has been corrected already by the bank. To exclude extreme cases of regulatory abstention, the law may impose sanctions on regulators who are derelict in carrying out their duties or may permit bank creditors to bring a claim for damages suffered as a result of gross negligence on the part of the regulator.[87]

There are provisions of banking law which leave the regulator no choice in the exercise of its authority and require it to take regulatory action. In *Switzerland*, for example, the banking law contains the following provision:

> When the bank regulator discovers violations of the law or other irregularities, it shall take the measures necessary to restore the rule of law and to remove the irregularities.[88]

The provision requires the regulator to do whatever is necessary to remedy the situation; if the provision would have used permissive language and would have said *may take the measures*, it would have permitted the regulator to abstain from corrective action altogether. The

---

[86] See Section 4 in this chapter.

[87] See Chapter II, Section 5, above, for a brief discussion of regulatory immunity from such claims.

[88] Article 23ter(1) of the Federal Law on Banks and Savings Banks.

exercise of regulatory authority to take regulatory action is made mandatory. However, the meaning of "other irregularities" is uncertain and the choice of regulatory action is discretionary. This means that the provision is not strictly mandatory. It would be strictly mandatory if the provision would precisely define the irregularities and measures referred to in the provision.

Strictly mandatory provisions of banking law are fairly rare. They are usually reserved for special situations, where it concerns a particular regulatory act to be done in narrowly defined circumstances. For instance, in *England*, the banking law requires the bank regulator to revoke a bank's banking license when a winding-up order has been made against the bank.[89]

The banking law may curtail the discretion of the bank regulator in exercising authority granted by the banking law by prescribing review procedures whereby the bank is notified of impending regulatory action and is afforded an opportunity to present its views to the regulator in a hearing before action is taken by the regulator. Such procedures have the effect of delaying a regulatory response to banking problems and thereby restricting the discretion of the regulator in determining the timing of the response. For cases where a delay in regulatory action caused by such procedures would have serious adverse effects on the bank concerned or even the banking system as a whole, the law often permits the regulator to act without prior notification or hearing, pending completion of the review procedures.[90]

Along similar lines, banking laws sometimes grant authority to take regulatory action by prescribing a graduated two-step approach. The first step usually consists of a guideline, recommendation, or order to the bank to correct a certain deficiency, often within a deadline specified by the regulator, while the second step consists of more rigorous action, such as the application of a sanction or taking control of the bank through provisional administration if the first step is not taken by the bank.[91] One would expect that, when a bank fails to comply

---

[89] Section 11(6)(a) of the Banking Act 1987.

[90] See for a discussion of these procedures Chapter II, Section 4, above.

[91] *Belgium*: Article 57(1) of the Law on the Statute and Supervision of Credit Institutions; *Canada*: Sections 485(3)(a) *juncto* 648(1.1) of the Bank Act; *France*: Articles 43 *juncto* 45 of Law No. 84-46 on the Activities and Supervision of Credit Institutions; *Germany*: Section 45(2) of the Law on the Credit System; *Luxembourg*: Article 59(1) and (2) of the Law of 1993 on the Financial Sector; *Netherlands*: Article 28(2) and (3) of the Law on Supervision of the Credit System.

with a guideline or order of the regulator, the law would require the regulator to follow up with stricter regulatory action. Instead, the banking law typically permits the exercise of the regulator's authority to respond to this failure and provides accordingly that the second step *may* be taken.[92] As noncompliance with a direction of the bank regulator is a serious matter that should not be disregarded by the regulator, it is difficult to understand why the exercise of the regulator's authority at the second level would not be mandatory. Flexibility can be built into a mandatory two-step approach by allowing extensions of the deadline for completion of remedial action under the first step, and by making the choice of remedial action imposed as a second step more or less discretionary.

The discretion of the bank regulator in taking action can be restricted by providing that the action may only be taken with judicial concurrence. Typical examples would be taking regulatory control of a bank through a provisional administrator or a receiver to be appointed by court order. Pursuant to such provisions, the regulator may not exercise its authority without judicial approval and regulatory discretion of decision making is shared between the regulator and the court.

The balance of discretionary power between the regulator and the court can be adjusted by statutory provision. For instance, if the law provides that judicial insolvency proceedings may be opened against a bank upon the application of a bank's creditors after consultation with the bank regulator,[93] most of the discretionary decision-making power rests with the court. However, by providing in the law that judicial insolvency proceedings may be opened against a bank only upon a petition from the bank regulator,[94] the balance of discretionary power can be tilted somewhat toward the bank regulator. If in this example the law would also provide that the inability to pay or the insolvency of the bank is to be determined exclusively by the bank regulator, the discretionary power of decision making would rest mostly with the regulator. In the last mentioned case, the court would not materially participate in the decision-making process. Its role would be limited to protecting the interests of the bank by reviewing the petition in the light of, *inter alia*, procedural requirements of the banking law and general principles of administrative law, for instance, to ascertain that

---

[92] See the provisions cited in footnote 91.

[93] *France*: Article 46-3 of Law No. 84-46 on the Activities and Supervision of Credit Institutions; *Netherlands*: Article 70 of the Law on Supervision of the Credit System.

[94] *Germany*: Section 46b of the Law on the Credit System.

the petition is not unreasonable in the circumstances. Even if it lacks discretionary power in the decision-making process, the judiciary can play an important role as watchdog over compliance with the rule of law by the bank regulator.

Grounds for Regulatory Action

Typically, banking law provisions granting authority to take regulatory action specify the concrete circumstances in which that authority may or must be exercised. Broad and vaguely defined grounds for regulatory action leave the regulator greater discretion in deciding whether the circumstances of a particular case before it come within the scope of its authority to act, than do narrow and precisely defined grounds for regulatory action. Thus, the degree of discretion to be granted to the bank regulator to take regulatory action can be more or less controlled through the statutory grounds on which such action may be taken.

Sometimes, broad and narrow grounds are found side by side in the same section of the banking law. For example, the banking law of *Australia* contains substantially the following provision:

> (1) The bank regulator may give a bank a direction of a kind specified in subsection (2) if the regulator considers that the bank has contravened a prudential regulation or a prudential standard, or the direction is necessary in the interests of depositors of the bank.[95]

The provision specifies two basic grounds for issuing a direction to a bank: (A) the bank has contravened a prudential regulation or a prudential standard; and (B) a direction of a kind specified in subsection (2) is necessary in the interests of depositors of the bank. The ground described under (A) is fairly narrow as there will not be much discretion involved in deciding whether a bank has or has not contravened the law, one would hope. The ground described under (B) is fairly broad and allows the regulator considerable discretion in deciding whether the interests of a bank's depositors require a direction of a kind specified in subsection (2).

There are banking law provisions that grant authority to the bank regulator to take regulatory action without specifying any ground. For

---

[95] Section 11CA(1) of the Banking Act 1959.

example, the banking law of *France* includes a provision that in substance reads as follows:

> The bank regulator may issue a recommendation to a bank to take appropriate measures to restore or strengthen its financial condition, to improve its management methods or to ensure that its organization is adequate for its activities or development objectives. The bank concerned must respond within two months by describing in detail the measures taken pursuant to that recommendation.[96]

Although the discretion of the regulator in deciding *in what circumstances* to issue the recommendation may seem unlimited, in practice, its discretion will be restricted by principles of administrative law dictating that regulatory action as permitted by the provision may not be taken without sufficient cause. In this context, it should be noted that, for obvious reasons, no mandatory provision of banking law was found that authorizes regulatory action without specifying the grounds on which such action must be taken.

Where the grounds for regulatory action set out in the banking law are broad, granting the regulator a broad measure of discretion, the regulator may be required by law to issue regulations that give more precise content to those grounds and better define the circumstances in which regulatory action may be taken.[97]

Choice of Regulatory Action

Finally, the law may adjust the degree of discretion to be granted to the bank regulator by listing the actions that the regulator may or must take. In doing so, the legislature may limit the choice of regulatory actions available to the regulator. This is a useful legislative technique to correlate certain regulatory measures with certain grounds for taking regulatory action. The technique is also used to specify certain categories of regulatory action that the regulator may take at its discretion, implicitly excluding other categories of measures that are not suitable for such discretionary treatment, such as measures that are so intrusive into the affairs of a bank that they should only be taken by the judiciary.

---

[96] Article 43 of Law No. 84-46 on the Activities and Supervision of Credit Institutions. Failure to respond may lead to punishment of the bank with a disciplinary sanction pursuant to Article 45 of Law No. 84-46.

[97] See, e.g., *United States*: 12 U.S.C. § 1831p–1 and 12 C.F.R. 30, and Chapter IV, Section 2, below, for a brief discussion of this technique.

The degree of statutory specificity in prescribing what regulatory action may be taken differs considerably from country to country, and in some countries from provision to provision of the banking law. At one end of the spectrum are broad provisions that authorize the regulator to take whatever measures are necessary to remedy the infractions referred to in the grounds for exercising the authority.[98] At the other end of the spectrum are banking law provisions with exhaustive lists of the kinds of regulatory action that may be taken.[99] There are also banking law provisions where the broad approach is combined with an illustrative list of measures.[100]

Some banking laws cover both ends of the scale in a single provision. Thus, for example, the banking law of *Australia* lists 14 kinds of direction that the regulator may give to a bank, including, *inter alia*:

    (f) a direction not to accept the deposit of any amount;

    (j) a direction not to pay a dividend on any shares;

    (n) any other direction as to the way in which the affairs of the bank are to be conducted or not conducted. [101]

The open-ended kind of direction last listed implicitly recognizes, and cures, the principal disadvantage attached to an exhaustive enumeration of regulatory action: as the legislature cannot foresee all kinds of measures that the bank regulator may need to respond adequately to the violation of evolving prudential standards, writing an exhaustive list of regulatory action into the law risks omitting the very measure that is needed.

Prompt Corrective Action in the United States

Some of the foregoing considerations may be illustrated by reference to the mandatory regulatory response of prompt corrective action that United States law imposes in case a bank fails to meet prudential capital adequacy standards.

The severe banking and savings and loan crises of the 1980s and suspicion that the crises had been worsened by lax banking supervision

---

[98] *Netherlands*: Article 14 of the Law on Supervision of the Credit System; *Switzerland*: Article 23ter (1) of the Federal Law on Banks and Savings Banks.

[99] *France*: Article 45 of Law No. 84-46 on the Activities and Supervision of Credit Institutions.

[100] *Germany*: Article 46 (1) of the Law on the Credit System.

[101] Section 11CA(2) of the Banking Act 1959.

led the U.S. Congress to adopt the FDIC Improvement Act of 1991. The Act includes under the heading "prompt corrective action" a relatively long and detailed list of violations and corresponding corrective measures that a bank is required to take or the bank regulator is required to order, based on the level of the bank's capital.[102] The provisions were designed to limit regulatory forbearance by requiring intervention that would be more timely and less discretionary, with the objective of reducing the costs of bank failures.[103]

Notwithstanding the impression of relative inflexibility that it was meant to create, the system of prompt corrective action is less mandatory in practice than its appearance would suggest. One reason is that the measures prescribed by the law have a degree of flexibility built into the text of the prescriptions that is necessary in practice to address the differing circumstances of different banking institutions. Thus, the system of prompt corrective action consists largely of requirements for banks to submit and carry out a capital restoration plan whose content is negotiated with the regulator, leaving considerable room for discretion as to the content of the plan.

Concluding Observations

In determining the scope of discretion to be granted to the bank regulator, balances must be struck in two partly overlapping areas, namely: (a) a balance between protecting the banking system as a whole and protecting the interests of individual banks and their owners through tightly written banking law provisions or judicial involvement; and (b) a balance between protecting the banking system from both regulatory abuse and negligent forbearance and the need to avoid provisions that are so tightly written that they would unduly impair the ability of the regulator to address unexpected conditions or unforeseen innovations in banking services or financial products.

The unprecedented rate of change in the financial markets and the banking industry experienced during the last decades has made it necessary to grant bank regulators greater regulatory discretion than previously was deemed desirable. This development has shifted the burden of providing safeguards against abuse of discretion to administrative law applied by an independent judiciary. Decisions as

---

[102] 12 U.S.C. § 1831o.
[103] FDIC, *History of the Eighties—Lessons for the Future*, 1997, Vol. 1 at p. 51.

to the degree of discretion to be granted to the bank regulator may depend on these and other considerations, including the extent of accountability and functional autonomy of the bank regulator.

Regulatory discretion means that for certain measures the legislature relies more or less on the regulator's judgment. In bank regulation, there are generally good reasons for doing so. The bank regulator must be assumed to have unique expertise and experience with regard to matters falling within its jurisdiction that justify making it solely responsible for decisions on those matters. Generally speaking, laws granting discretion to the bank regulator are testimonials that the legislature has confidence in the regulator, whereas laws that are mandatory or otherwise prescriptive reflect a lack of trust in the regulator.[104]

While a discretionary regime preserves flexibility for the regulator, it may create uncertainty concerning regulatory action. Moreover, a discretionary regulatory framework may raise concerns about the fairness of regulatory intervention, especially in countries where respect for the rule of administrative law on the part of the regulator is wanting. In contrast, while a mandatory regime is relatively inflexible, it offers greater transparency and certainty about regulatory action than a discretionary regime, and it promotes equality of treatment. As was suggested before, the transparency and predictability of a discretionary regime may be enhanced by issuing definitions of circumstances that would trigger the authority of the regulator to take action.[105]

The principal weakness of a strictly mandatory system is its methodology of eliminating regulatory discretion and prescribing in its stead uniform measures for all banks that have reached a certain state of noncompliance with the banking law, regardless of whether such measures are appropriate in the light of prevailing circumstances. A prescriptive regime of regulatory action that is too strictly mandatory puts the bank regulator into a straightjacket and may exclude or impede a flexible response. Theoretically, under extreme circumstances, a mandatory corrective system rigidly applied could produce a wholesale closure of the banking system. Such an outcome would violate the elementary objective of prudential banking regulation aiming at the preservation of a functioning banking system. Therefore, a mandatory regime may force the regulator, when faced by conditions unforeseen

---

[104] The latter is illustrated by the legislative history of the prompt corrective action law in the United States that was briefly described in the foregoing section.

[105] See, e.g., *United States*: 12 U.S.C. § 1831p-1 and 12 C.F.R. 30, and Chapter IV, Section 2, below, for a brief discussion of these provisions.

by the legislature, either to order measures that are not suitable for the problems to be corrected or to avoid taking the action prescribed by the law altogether—for instance, by denying that a statutory ground for the action exists—and thus to break the law. Obviously, this dilemma should be avoided.

Under certain conditions a strictly mandatory regime should be ruled out *a priori*. For instance, a strictly mandatory regime is generally unsuitable for heterogeneous banking systems, because these banking systems require a fair degree of corrective differentiation by the regulator, owing to differences in the conditions and needs of various categories of banks. Similarly, mandatory banking law provisions whose application depends on a valuation of marketable bank assets should be avoided in countries with less developed or illiquid financial markets that do not produce reliable asset values.

Logic dictates, therefore, that even a mandatory regime normally requires a minimum of discretion for the bank regulator. Such discretion may be provided by the law in the form of exceptions to mandatory provisions in order to address unusual circumstances.[106] Exceptions can be made to the regulatory action required, to the grounds on which such action must be taken, or to both. However, where such exceptions undermine the objectives pursued in making the regime mandatory, they would normally be permitted only if the result of the application of the mandatory regime in a particular case would be incompatible with crucial systemic interests or would otherwise be patently unreasonable.

Does a mandatory regime moderated by suitable exceptions produce better results than one that is discretionary? It cannot be denied that discretion can easily turn into permissiveness and lax banking supervision, especially in societies with a club culture. In contrast, a mandatory regime creates an appearance of predictability and equality of treatment and thereby enhances the credibility of the bank regulator.[107] Mandatory systems of regulatory action have other advantages. These are chiefly that they require frequent monitoring of the bank

---

[106] See also Section 2.3.3 of the Report of the G-22 Working Group on Strengthening Financial Systems.

[107] In some countries with emerging market economies, the certainties provided by a mandatory regime with firm statutory rules would compensate for a lack of trained bank regulators. In such countries, a mandatory system could also help keep the judiciary from reviewing discretionary decisions of bank regulators as to their merits and overturning them.

and that, even though applying their trigger points may be more an art than a science, they force regulators periodically to collect and analyze evidence concerning the direction in which the bank's financial condition develops.

It may be concluded from the foregoing that a good banking law would generally require the bank regulator promptly to take appropriate action to address violations of prudential standards by a bank, and would empower the regulator to do so by offering a balanced menu of options representing both a discretionary and a moderately mandatory approach, depending on the kinds of circumstance addressed, while generally submitting the most invasive regulatory measures to a prior review by the judiciary. For each country, its sociopolitical character and its experience with banking crises will help determine whether its banking law grants more or less discretion to the bank regulator in addressing banking problems.

3. Gradation of Regulatory Intervention

In considering the degree of discretion to be granted to the bank regulator, it is not unusual to find an inverse relationship between the generality of the grounds for authority to take corrective action and the variety or invasiveness of corrective action allowed to be taken under that authority. It is not uncommon for the law to combine broad grounds of authority with narrowly prescribed corrective actions and narrow grounds of authority with broader arrays of measures. Similarly, some banking laws show a tendency toward more narrowly defined grounds of authority as the action that they authorize becomes more invasive. Examples of these tendencies are found in countries where the banking law grants the regulator discretionary authority to issue orders or restrictions concerning a bank's activities while requiring a court order for taking control of a bank through a receivership.[108]

In line with this practice, it has been recommended that countries adopt, implement, and enforce a method of structured early intervention in the banking sector that includes a well-considered set of mechanisms to ensure a consistent, timely, and graduated response by supervisors.[109]

---

[108] E.g., *Australia, Austria, Canada, Germany, Netherlands.*

[109] Recommendation in the G-22 Working Group Report on Strengthening Financial Systems, at page (vii) and section 2.3.3.

As a graduated approach to regulatory intervention is a logical extension of the administrative law principle of proportionality, examples of a graduated response can be found in many banking laws.

For instance, regulatory action must be graduated where the banking law requires the regulator to follow a two-step approach, the first step consisting of a guideline, order, or recommendation issued to the bank to correct a certain deficiency within a certain deadline, followed by a second step of more rigorous regulatory action in the event of an inadequate response by the bank to the first step.[110]

The Banking Act 1959 of *Australia* offers another example. Regulatory intervention authorized by the Act falls into two categories: the regulator may by notice in writing give "directions" to a bank; or the regulator may appoint an investigator or take direct or indirect control of the business of a bank. The grounds on which these two kinds of action may be taken differ.

A "direction" may be given by the regulator if the regulator considers that the bank has contravened a prudential regulation or a prudential standard, or that the direction is necessary in the interests of depositors of the bank.[111] The kinds of directions that may be given are specified by the Act; they include directions to comply with a certain prudential standard, directions to remove, suspend, or replace managers, directions to desist from any borrowing, payment, or transfer, and directions generally to conduct or not to conduct the affairs of the bank in any way.[112] Sanctions on noncompliance with a direction include criminal penalties levied against the bank and noncomplying bank officers,[113] and publication of the direction.[114]

If the bank regulator considers that a bank is likely to become unable to meet its obligations or is about to suspend payment or if a bank

---

[110] *Belgium*: Article 57(1) of the Law on the Statute and Supervision of Credit Institutions; *Canada*: Sections 485(3)(a) *juncto* 648(1.1) of the Bank Act; *France*: Articles 43 *juncto* 45 of Law No. 84-46 on the Activities and Supervision of Credit Institutions; *Germany*: Section 45(2) of the Law on the Credit System; *Luxembourg*: Article 59(1) and (2) of the Law of 1993 on the Financial Sector; *Netherlands*: Article 28(2) and (3) of the Law on Supervision of the Credit System. See also the discussion in Section 2, above.

[111] Section 11CA(1) of the Banking Act 1959.

[112] Section 11CA(2) of the Banking Act 1959.

[113] Section 11CG of the Banking Act 1959.

[114] Section 11CE(1) of the Banking Act 1959. Although publication is perhaps not a sanction in a formal sense, it may be practically more significant than the levy of penalties, because publication of a direction will often adversely affect the bank's reputation and therefore increase its funding costs.

becomes unable to meet its obligations or suspends payment, the regulator may appoint a person to investigate the affairs of the bank, take control of the bank's business or appoint an administrator to take control of the bank's business.[115]

The difference in grounds is striking: whereas the general ground for giving directions to a bank is its noncompliance with prudential law or regulations, the more intrusive corrective actions of appointment of an investigator and taking control of the bank are reserved for cases where the bank is or is about to become illiquid or insolvent.

One of the problems posed by a graduated approach is that it requires the grading of violations of prudential law and regulatory responses thereto on a single scale of abstract values. Although such grading may be possible for certain broad categories of violation, it is ill-suited to others. For instance, although deficiencies in the financial condition of a bank, such as a bank's failure to meet capital adequacy requirements, could be scaled because they have effects that can be measured in numerical terms, it will be difficult to bring these financial infractions under a common denominator with other offences, such as money laundering, that cannot be so measured.

The graduated approach to regulatory action addresses the proportionality between violations of prudential law and regulatory responses thereto. Regulatory action is ratcheted up or down as banking law violations by a bank become more or less serious. This should not be taken to imply that the bank regulator must first exhaust lesser corrective remedies before more intrusive regulatory measures may be taken. Although there are cases where a regimen of measures of increasing severity would clearly be appropriate, there also are situations where the regulator would wish to address simultaneously different types of deficiencies with different types of measures graded at different points on the scale, such as capital inadequacies requiring the bank to recapitalize and managerial incompetence or crookedness requiring the replacement of managers. Also, the fact that a particular measure is more intrusive than another one does not necessarily mean that it should be postponed until a less invasive measure has been tried first; for example, although the appointment of a provisional administrator is relatively invasive, it may be the only action that is appropriate to replace a crooked management until a new management has been appointed by the owners.[116]

---

[115] Section 13A(1) of the Banking Act 1959.
[116] See for this case *Germany*, Article 46 of the Law on the Credit System.

Much more cannot be said about a graduated response than that corrective action should be tailored to the deficiencies encountered and that corrective action should neither go beyond what is necessary to return the bank to full compliance with prudential requirements nor be too weak to achieve its goal.

4. Timeliness of Regulatory Measures

To be effective, corrective regulatory action must be swift and decisive. In contrast, experience would seem to point to a widespread tendency on the part of bank regulators to postpone effective action against wayward banks. The history of prudential regulation of banks is replete with instances of regulatory forbearance with respect to banks that the regulator knew to be in difficulty. Whether it is the savings and loan crisis of the 1980s in the United States, the problems of Crédit Lyonnais, BCCI, or Barings, or the more recent banking crises in Korea, Russia, Thailand, and Indonesia, some of the blame for these events has been laid at the doorstep of the bank regulator.

There are situations, of course, where regulatory forbearance is justified, for instance, when the banking sector is overwhelmed by adverse economic conditions and the regulator must respond by relaxing prudential requirements, provided that this is done explicitly and publicly and applies to all banks alike. Often, however, regulatory forbearance is a serious problem, especially when it consists of negligence of the regulator in its main task, namely, to identify and respond to banking problems before they spin out of control; then, regulatory forbearance can undermine the entire bank regulatory structure. Although some of the causes of regulatory negligence are known—political interference in the regulatory process and a club culture are among them—a thorough analysis (which would go beyond the scope of this book) might show why this phenomenon is so widespread and what should be done to curtail it.

Negligent forbearance by the bank regulator carries significant costs. Not surprisingly, it leads to banking problems, which cause increases in costs for bank creditors in case of bank failures, and for the monetary authorities in case of bank rescue operations. Generally, regulatory negligence is inequitable as it produces unfair competition: banks not complying with prudential regulations are allowed to avoid costs associated with regulatory compliance and are therefore permitted to operate from a lower regulatory cost base than banks that are in compliance. Worse for the banking system is that regulatory negligence breeds a culture of noncompliance with banking law. Compliance with banking law cannot be assured without the voluntary cooperation of bankers; because regulatory negligence permits some banks to disregard the banking law, it creates a powerful incentive for all banks to do likewise, leading eventually to widespread deficiencies in the banking system. In the end, regulatory negligence regarding banks that the public perceives as weak undermines the credibility of the bank regulator, creates uncertainties for the public concerning the financial condition of all banks, and thus heightens systemic risk.

Developments in the business of the banking industry over the last two decades have worsened the risks attending corrective action unduly postponed. Changes in consumer investment preferences have forced many banks to replace their traditional deposit base with money market instruments. Also, the income of banks derives increasingly from financial services requiring transactions with other financial institutions. The financial markets are more sensitive to negative publicity concerning a bank than most depositors were in the past. As a result of the information revolution, news reaches financial market participants faster than before, and their reaction to such news is faster than a traditional run on a bank by depositors would be.

The shortened reaction time of bank counterparties should cause regulators likewise to react to banking irregularities faster than before. The longer corrective action is postponed, the more forceful it generally will be, increasing the risks of a violent market reaction. The provisions of U.S. law requiring banks in distress and the regulator to take prompt corrective action[117] have been written with this consideration in mind to promote an early and proportional corrective response to banking deficiencies.

5. Reporting and Disclosure Requirements

Financial reporting is the Achilles' heel of the bank regulator. Without adequate information about a bank's noncompliance with prudential standards, the bank regulator will not be able to order corrective action as and when needed. Much touted market discipline in keeping banks on the straight and narrow depends on timely and adequate reports on the financial condition of banks. As a rule, therefore, banks are subject to regular reporting requirements or on-site inspec-

---

[117] 12 U.S.C. § 1831o.

tions by the regulator. In addition, banks whose capital shares or debt securities are publicly traded usually must disclose to the public significant changes in their financial condition.

In some countries, the law requires a bank or its management or auditors to alert the bank regulator if it is likely to become unable to meet its obligations or is about to suspend payments,[118] or if it becomes insolvent or overindebted.[119] For example, in *Norway*, the law requires the bank, its managers, and auditors to notify the regulator:

> if there is reason to fear that:
>
> a) the institution may be unable to meet its commitments as they fall due,
>
> b) the institution may be unable to meet the minimum requirements as to its own funds or other capital adequacy and prudential requirements set out in law or regulations,
>
> c) circumstances have arisen that may entail a serious loss of confidence or losses that will substantially weaken or threaten the institution's financial position.[120]

Often, when an instance of noncompliance with prudential requirements is uncovered by the bank regulator there are reasons to fear that what became visible is merely the tip of the proverbial iceberg. For such cases, the law may authorize the regulator to order a special audit of the bank covering not only its financial condition but also its operations and risk management policies and procedures, or to appoint an observer.[121]

As was noted before, the increasing exposure of banks to financial market risks and the communication revolution have reduced the reaction time of bank counterparties to real or perceived weaknesses in a bank's financial condition. This requires improved flows of information from the banks to the regulator that permit the regulator to form faster judgments about the current financial condition and risk exposure of the banks. In particular, the time lags implicit in traditional forms of information gathering by bank regulators should be significantly shortened, for instance, by giving the regulator electronic access

---

[118] *Australia*: Section 13(3) of the Banking Act 1959.

[119] *Germany*: Section 46b of the Law on the Credit System.

[120] Section 3-1(1) of the Law on Guarantee Schemes for Banks, 1996. The notification must contain information on the bank's liquidity and capital condition and explain the reasons for the difficulties—Section 3-1(3).

[121] See Chapter V, Section 3, below.

to accounting data of banks that reflect each bank's unique risk profile and risk management. Real-time banking supervision would help the regulator to take early and therefore limited action that would not attract undue public attention.

6. Financial Costs of Regulatory Intervention

For the bank regulator, there are financial costs or expenses associated with regulatory intervention. As these activities are often labor intensive and a drain on its staff and other resources, the law may allow the regulator to recoup these costs and expenses.

This is especially important for situations where the intervention costs to the regulator are significant, as they would be when the regulator would take control of a bank through a provisional administrator or a receiver. If the costs of a successful regulatory rescue mission are not recouped, the bank and its owners would enjoy an unfair benefit in comparison with other banks. In order to avoid that such a bank and its owners would become "free riders" at the expense of the regulator, it is important that the bank should bear the financial costs incurred by the regulator on account of the restructuring of the bank. The banking law may make provision for charging the expenses of regulatory intervention to the bank [122] and grant to the regulator the powers necessary to enforce its right to reimbursement on account of such expenses, for instance, by granting it a statutory preference in the bank's liquidation.[123]

---

[122] *Canada*: Section 654 of the Bank Act; *Germany*: Article 51(3) of the Law on the Credit System; *Netherlands*: Article 86 of the Law on Supervision of the Credit System.
[123] *Canada*: Section 655 of the Bank Act.

Principal Objectives To Be Pursued by Law

The law should require the bank regulator to respond promptly and adequately to infractions of prudential standards and should grant the bank regulator a degree of discretion of decision making that is commensurate with the need for a proper response to unpredictable conditions in the banking system. Even mandatory regimes prescribing corrective action should afford the regulator sufficient discretion to take account of unforeseen conditions.

Regulatory action to correct banking deficiencies should be broadly gradual, in consonance with the administrative law principle of proportionality. Such action should be taken in a timely fashion so as to avoid that stricter measures would be required later, and so as to maintain a level regulatory playing field for all banks.

Financial reporting by banks to the regulator should be improved so as to give the regulator continuous real-time information about the bank's financial condition.

Banks should reimburse the regulator for the regulator's costs and expenses on account of measures taken to correct deficiencies in their compliance with prudential regulations; free ridership of owners of banks benefiting from corrective action should be precluded.

IV

Corrective Action: Common Features

1. Authority to Take Corrective Action

In defining the authority of the regulator to order corrective action, most laws use permissive language and provide that the regulator *may* order the bank to take corrective measures. Some provisions of banking law, however, use mandatory language in providing remedial authority, requiring the regulator to take corrective action whenever a particular infraction has occurred and is continuing or a level of noncompliance described in the law has been reached.[124]

Sometimes, the law reinforces the authority of the regulator. In one country, the banking law contains the following provision:

> Where, notwithstanding a prior warning, an enforceable decision of the Banking Commission is not observed within the deadline specified, the Banking Commission may itself , but for the account of the noncomplying bank, take the measures that it had ordered.[125]

In another country, the law permits the regulator to apply for a court order requiring the bank to comply with the regulator's instructions.[126]

Alternatively, the law may authorize the bank regulator to impose fines[127] or other sanctions[128] for not complying with prudential

---

[124] See, for a discussion of this distinction, Chapter III, Section 2, above.

[125] *Switzerland*: Article 23ter(2) of the Federal Law on Banks and Savings Banks.

[126] *Canada*: Section 646 of the Bank Act.

[127] *Australia*: Section 11CG of the Banking Act 1959; *Belgium*: Article 103 of the Law on the Statute and Supervision of Credit Institutions; *England*: Sections 44, 81, and 94 of the Banking Act 1987; *France*: Articles 75 ff. of Law No. 84-46 on the Activities and Supervision of Credit Institutions; *Germany*: Articles 54–56 of the Law on the Credit System.

[128] *France*: Article 45 of Law No. 84-46 on the Activities and Supervision of Credit Institutions.

requirements or orders of the bank regulator. The exercise of this power by the regulator may violate international human rights if sanctions are imposed without a court of law.[129] In *France*, the law provides that when the bank regulator imposes a sanction it is an administrative court, which as such must comply with certain procedural requirements designed to safeguard the legitimate interests of defendants, including the right to a fair and public hearing.[130]

The authority to order corrective measures goes hand in hand with the responsibility to impose the right corrective measures. Imposing the wrong measures may damage the bank for which they are taken, or may impair the regulator's reputation and ultimately its credibility. Moreover, the more invasive corrective action is, the greater is the risk for the regulator that incorrect or ineffective measures will do more harm than good and create liability toward the bank concerned.

2. Grounds for Taking Corrective Action

In prescribing the grounds for corrective action, banking laws follow different patterns. Some banking law provisions follow a broad approach, prescribing generic grounds. Others follow a narrow approach and link specific authority to take certain corrective measures to one or more specified circumstances.

A good example of the broad approach is the variety of grounds specified in the banking law of *Belgium*, including that the bank is not operating in accordance with the provisions of the banking law and its implementing decrees and regulations, that the bank's management policy or its financial position is likely to prevent it from honoring its commitments or fails to offer sufficient guarantees for its solvency, liquidity, or profitability, or that its management structure, administrative and accounting procedures, or internal control systems present serious deficiencies.[131] In the *Netherlands*, the banking law authorizes corrective action if the regulator determines that the bank fails to comply with the regulator's directions concerning the bank's solvency, liquidity, or administrative organization or if the regulator discovers signs of a devel-

---

[129] See, e.g., Articles 10 and 11 of the Universal Declaration of Human Rights; and Article 6 of the European Convention for the Protection of Human Rights and Fundamental Freedoms.

[130] Article 48 of Law No. 84-46 on the Activities and Supervision of Credit Institutions.

[131] *Belgium*: Article 57 (1) of the Law on the Statute and Supervision of Credit Institutions.

opment that in its judgment endangers or could endanger the solvency or liquidity of the bank.[132]

A threat to the interests of a bank's depositors is a common ground for corrective action. For instance, in *England*, one of the grounds for taking corrective action is that it appears to the regulator that "the interests of depositors or potential depositors of the institution are in any ... way threatened, whether by the manner in which the institution is conducting or proposes to conduct its affairs or for any other reason."[133] Similarly, though more broadly, the banking law may prescribe that the bank's ability to meet its obligations toward its creditors is endangered.[134]

Another example of the broad approach is the following ground for corrective action found in the banking law of *Canada*:

> ... in the opinion of the Superintendent, a bank, or a person with respect to a bank, is committing, or is about to commit, an act that is an unsafe or unsound practice in conducting the business of the bank, or is pursuing or is about to pursue any course of conduct that is an unsafe or unsound practice in conducting the business of the bank ...[135]

Alternatively, the law may require that the bank "contravened a law or regulation relating to its business" before disciplinary sanctions are imposed.[136] A somewhat extreme example of discretion is found in the statutory ground granting the bank regulator authority to take corrective action when the regulator is of the opinion that it is in the public interest to do so.[137]

---

[132] *Netherlands*: Article 28 (1) of the Law on Supervision of the Credit System.

[133] Section 11(1)(e) of the Banking Act 1987. See further for the use of depositors' interest as a ground for corrective action, *Austria*: Article 70(2) of the Banking Act; *Canada*: Section 648(1.1)(b), (c), and (e) of the Bank Act; *Germany*: Section 46(1) of the Law on the Credit System.

[134] *Austria*: Article 70(2) of the Austrian Banking Act; *Canada*: Section 648(1.1)((b), (c), and (e) of the Bank Act; *Germany*: Section 46(1) of the Law on the Credit System.

[135] Section 645(1) of the Bank Act. Cf. *France*: Article 42 of Law No. 84-46 on the Activities and Supervision of Credit Institutions; *United States*: 12 U.S.C. § 1818(b)(1).

[136] *France*: Article 45 of Law No. 84-46 on the Activities and Supervision of Credit Institutions.

[137] *Ireland*: Section 21 (1) of the Central Bank Act; see also *Australia*: Section 9A(2)(b) of the Banking Act 1959 authorizing the revocation of the authority to carry on banking business in Australia if the regulator is satisfied that "it would be contrary to the national interest for the authority to remain in force."

As explained before,[138] the broader the statutory grounds are for taking corrective action, the more discretion the bank regulator has in deciding that there are grounds for taking corrective action in a particular case. Therefore, broad grounds for corrective action create greater uncertainties for banks concerning the meaning and scope of the prudential standards protected by the statutory provisions concerned, and are more apt to raise doubts concerning the evenhandedness of bank regulators, than narrow grounds. To mitigate these disadvantages, the bank regulator may issue regulations giving specific content to some of the broader grounds for corrective action that are found in the banking law.

Thus, for instance, in the *United States*, where corrective action is authorized on the ground that a bank engages in an unsafe or unsound practice in conducting its business,[139] the bank regulator has issued safety and soundness standards as well as procedures for their enforcement.[140] This approach has several advantages. The banks are informed about the standards of banking practice and the procedures that the bank regulator will apply in determining whether a bank is in violation of the banking law. The standards are marginal standards defining the boundaries of tolerable banking practices; within these boundaries the banks are free; nevertheless, within the framework of its general supervision activities, the bank regulator should caution banks that are found moving close to the border line. By further defining the grounds for taking corrective action, the regulator reduces its discretion, while creating an expectation that the standards will be enforced, promoting predictability of regulatory action and enhancing its public credibility.

Some banking law provisions follow a narrower approach, for instance, by enumerating fairly precisely the circumstances in which a particular corrective measure may be taken. [141] A disadvantage of the narrow approach is that the legislature may overlook some worthwhile targets and leave them uncovered—for example, when the law addresses deficiencies in the financial condition of banks, while omitting other types of infractions, such as money laundering and other criminal activities. It is possible of course to cover bank crimes elsewhere in the law.

---

[138] Chapter III, Section 2, above.
[139] 12 U.S.C. § 1818(b)(1).
[140] 12 U.S.C. § 1831p-1 and 12 C.F.R. 30.
[141] *Netherlands*: Articles 20, 21, and 22 of the Law on Supervision of the Credit System.

3. Corrective Action Plans

It is difficult to exaggerate the importance of the adoption and execution of a good corrective action plan. The outline of such action plans are given in the following example.

The law may require that a bank whose regulatory capital is insufficient submit to the bank regulator a capital restoration plan describing the steps that the bank will take to become adequately capitalized, the levels of capital to be attained during each year that the plan will be in effect, how the bank will comply with other corrective measures ordered by the regulator, and the types and levels of activities in which the bank will engage. The law may also specify standards that a capital restoration plan must meet before it may be accepted by the bank regulator; these may include that the plan is based on realistic assumptions, that it is likely to succeed in restoring the bank's capital, and that it would not appreciably increase the risk to which the institution is exposed.[142] Finally, the law may require corrective action plans to include standards by which the effects of the plan's corrective measures on the bank's condition are to be evaluated.

Although often corrective action plans may be unilaterally imposed by the regulator, sometimes the law requires that they be more or less negotiated between the regulator and the bank, taking the form of a plan submitted by the bank to the regulator for its acceptance.[143]

A negotiated corrective action plan has several advantages. It provides a consensual framework for corrective measures that is not merely imposed by the regulator from above but that is designed by or together with the bank concerned, promoting "ownership" in the plan on the part of the bank's management and owners and minimizing responsibility of the bank regulator for its failure. It establishes discipline in identifying the needs of the bank, in designing the remedies responsive to those needs, in determining in detail the corrective measures required and the timetable for taking them, and in estimating the effects of the plan on the future condition of the bank. Finally, the plan offers an agenda for consultations between the bank and the reg-

---

[142] *United States*: 12 U.S.C. § 1831o(e)(2). Although this is not required by law, it is common practice in the United States for the bank regulator to negotiate with banks in distress cease and desist orders containing detailed plans of corrective measures.

[143] *Argentina*: Article 34 of the Financial Institutions Law; *United States*: 12 U.S.C. § 1831o(e)(2).

ulator on adjustments to corrective measures as conditions change during the execution of the plan.

For these reasons, it is not difficult to see how a plan of action can help ensure the success of corrective measures. Unfortunately, however, corrective action plans do not figure prominently in banking laws.

V

Corrective Action: Categories

1. Choice of Corrective Action

The same two legislative approaches that were identified with respect to the grounds for corrective action apply to the choice of corrective action.

Some banking laws contain broad provisions that leave the choice of corrective measures largely to the bank regulator. For example, in *Australia,* the law authorizes the bank regulator to impose on a bank, at any time, by written notice, conditions on the bank's authority to carry on banking business in Australia; the conditions must relate to matters relating to the conduct by the bank of any of its affairs: (a) in such a way as to keep the bank in a sound financial position and not to cause or promote instability in the Australian financial system; and (b) with integrity, prudence, and financial skill.[144] However, the law of *Australia* also includes narrowly defined corrective measures: when the bank regulator decides to issue a direction to a bank, it must make a choice from among 14 different kinds of direction specified by the law.[145]

Alternatively, the banking law may grant the bank regulator broad authority to issue orders directing a bank to cease and desist from any unsafe or unsound practice in conducting its business or to take appropriate remedial action.[146] In contrast, the banking law may restrict the use of certain corrective measures to certain deficiencies that they are designed to cure.[147]

---

[144] Sections 9(4) *juncto* Section 5 of the Banking Act 1959; it should be noted that Australian law does not expressly limit the exercise of this authority to situations where the bank concerned has violated the standards listed by the provision. Cf. *England:* Section 12(2) of the Banking Act 1987.

[145] Section 11CA of the Banking Act 1959.

[146] *Canada:* Section 645(1) of the Bank Act; *England:* Section 12(4)(a) of the Banking Act 1987; *Netherlands:* Article 28(2) of the Law on Supervision of the Credit System; *Switzerland:* Article 23ter(1) of the Federal Law on Banks and Savings Banks; *United States:* 12 U.S.C. § 1818(b) and (c).

[147] *Canada:* Sections 480 and 485 of the Bank Act.

Some banking laws combine broad grounds on which corrective action may be taken with a narrow choice of actions enumerated in the law.[148] For instance, the banking law of *Portugal* provides that when a bank is in a "financially unbalanced situation" the bank regulator may chose one or more carefully defined categories of corrective measures, including, *inter alia*, presentation of a financial reorganization plan and restrictions on the taking of deposits.[149]

Conversely, other banking laws combine narrowly defined grounds on which corrective action may be taken with a broad choice of actions. For example, in the *Netherlands*, when a bank fails to comply with any of five requirements specified in the banking law, the regulator may "direct the competent organs of the credit institution to follow a particular course of action in order to achieve compliance... ."[150]

Obviously, the more accurately a corrective measure targets a violation of the banking law, the greater the chance will be that the measure will achieve its objective. However, the law is a crude instrument to accomplish this goal as it is difficult for the legislator to predict all banking problems that may arise. Moreover, to be effective, the regulator must be able to provide a flexible response to the changing nature and circumstances of banking problems. Therefore, even though limiting the grounds for, or the choice of, corrective action in the law provides some legal certainty, its cost in flexibility must be deemed too great.

In addition to the foregoing, the law may require or authorize the bank regulator to order the bank to return to compliance with prudential standards by a certain deadline.[151] One banking law even provides that, if the bank fails to heed the order, the regulator may itself take the measure ordered, at the expense of the delinquent bank.[152]

Corrective action may take the form of a limitation or a condition attached to the banking license. What in some countries would be the

---

[148] *Australia*: Section 11CA(1)(b) and (2) of the Banking Act 1959; *Luxembourg*: Article 59(2) of the Law of 1993 on the Financial Sector; *Portugal*: Article 141 of the Legal Framework of Credit Institutions and Financial Companies, approved by Decree-Law No. 298/92.

[149] Article 141 of the Legal Framework of Credit Institutions and Financial Companies, approved by Decree-Law No. 298/92.

[150] Article 14 of the Law on Supervision of the Credit System.

[151] *Belgium*: Article 57(1) of the Law on the Statute and Supervision of Credit Institutions; *France*: Article 43 of Law No. 84-46 on the Activities and Supervision of Credit Institution; *Netherlands*: Article 14 of the Law on Supervision of the Credit System; *Portugal*: Article 141 of the Legal Framework of Credit Institutions and Financial Companies, approved by Decree-Law No. 298/92.

[152] *Switzerland*: Article 23ter(2) of the Federal Law on Banks and Savings Banks.

authority to order corrective action is in other countries the power of the bank regulator to restrict the banking license, by imposing such limit on its duration as the regulator thinks fit, or by imposing such conditions as it thinks desirable for the protection of the institution's depositors or potential depositors, or by the imposition of both such a limit and such conditions.[153]

Is the regulator generally authorized to threaten a bank with license revocation in order to force the bank into compliance? Unless license revocation would be a remedy that would be disproportional to the infraction addressed, threats of such action would seem permissible, especially if in doing so the regulator merely repeats the threat of regulatory action implicit in the law and thereby pursues the compliance goals of the law. The law of *England* underscores the need for proportionality in wielding this power, by directing the regulator to restrict a banking license instead of revoking the license if it appears to the regulator that there are grounds on which the regulator's power to revoke the license are exercisable but the circumstances are not such as to justify revocation.[154]

2. Corrective Agreements, Warnings, and Orders

In carrying out prudential supervision, bank regulators often discover a deficiency in a bank's operations or financial condition that, if not addressed, could develop into problems. Normally, the bank regulator would inform the bank of the deficiency and may even recommend remedial action to the bank.

Up to this point, the comments of the bank regulator about a bank's condition and its compliance with prudential banking standards would be regarded as part of ongoing banking supervision and would typically be included in supervision reports, without requiring special authority under the law.

Written Agreements

If the bank would not comply with the regulator's notice of deficiencies or recommendation for remedial action, the regulator may seek a

---

[153] *England*: Section 12(2) of the Banking Act 1987; see also *Australia*: Section 9(4) of the Banking Act 1959.

[154] Section 12(1) of the Banking Act 1987; the restrictions may consist of a time limit on the license of up to three years and conditions desirable for the protection of the bank's present and future depositors—Sections 12(2) and (3).

written agreement with the bank that would detail the bank's infractions of banking law and include a corrective action plan.[155] The chief advantages of such agreements are that they form an excellent consensual instrument for recording a bank's shortcomings in complying with prudential standards and the corrective actions that the bank with the consent of the regulator must take (corrective action plan), and that they provide a firm legal foundation for further corrective action if needed.

Warnings

At any stage, if a bank would not adequately respond to the regulator's advice or recommendations, the regulator may issue a warning to the bank that, unless adequate steps are taken by the bank to cure the deficiency, the regulator may have to resort to more invasive corrective action. Whenever the law attaches legal consequences to the failure of a bank to heed a warning by the regulator, explicit statutory authority to give the warning would seem to be required and the grounds on which a warning may be given may have to be specified in the law. Thus, in *France*, the law authorizes the bank regulator to issue a warning to a bank that has failed to follow sound banking practices, after having afforded the bank's management an opportunity to provide an explanation; if the warning is not taken into account, the bank regulator may impose a sanction.[156]

Measures Affecting Rights of Managers and Owners

The banking law may authorize the regulator to order meetings with the bank's management or owners to agree on corrective measures;[157]

---

[155] This is the practice in the *United States*: 12 U.S.C. § 1818(b)(1); even though the law does not provide explicit authority, Section 1818(b)(1) implicitly grants the regulator the power to enter into such written agreements without consideration by providing that a cease and desist order may issue upon any violation of such agreement. See Macey and Miller, *Banking Law and Regulation*, second edition (New York: Aspen Law and Business), 1997, at pp. 575–76.

[156] *France*: Articles 42 *juncto* 45 of Law No 84-46 on the Activities and Supervision of Credit Institutions.

[157] *France*: Article 52 of Law No. 84-46 on the Activities and Supervision of Credit Institutions provides that, when justified by a bank's condition, the Governor of the Bank of France, as chairman of the Banking Commission, calls upon the owners of the bank to provide the latter with the support it needs. The owners may refuse without liability; Christian Gavalda, and Jean Stoufflet, *Droit Bancaire*, fourth edition, at No.146; Sophie Grenouilloux, and Edouard Fernandez-Bollo, "France," in *International Bank Insolvencies: A Central Bank's Perspective*," ed. by Mario Giovanoli and Gregor Heinrich (The Hague: Kluwer Law International), 1999, at p. 60.

to direct the bank to remove managers of the bank;[158] to prohibit managers to carry out their duties in whole or in part;[159] to appoint a manager[160] or a substitute manager[161] to the bank; to prohibit dividend payments;[162] or to order an increase in the bank's capital.[163]

If owners, especially those who exercise control over a bank, refuse to cooperate with the bank regulator, the law should permit countermeasures designed to neutralize their power. These measures may include suspension of the voting rights of uncooperative owners by order of the bank regulator;[164] the appointment by court order of a trustee to exercise shareholder voting rights;[165] and a court order requiring owners to dispose of their shareholdings.[166] Ultimately, it may be necessary to place the bank under provisional administration or receivership,[167] in order that the provisional administrator or receiver may succeed to the powers of the bank's owners,[168] or may veto decision of owners;[169] or may require that the owners exercise their powers only following his prior consent and taking account of his instructions.[170]

---

[158] *Australia*: Section 11CA(2)(c)(i) of the Banking Act 1959; *Belgium*: Article 57(1)3 of the Law on the Statute and Supervision of Credit Institutions; *England*: Section 19(2)(e) of the Banking Act 1987; *Germany*: Section 35 of the Law on the Credit System.

[159] *Australia*: Section 11CA(2)(c)(ii) of the Banking Act 1959; *Austria*: Article 70(2)3 of the Austrian Banking Act; *Germany*: Section 46(1) of the Law on the Credit System; *Luxembourg*: Article 59(2)(a) of the Law on the Financial Sector.

[160] *Australia*: Section 11CA(2)(c)(iii) of the Banking Act 1959.

[161] *Belgium*: Article 57(1)3 of the Law on the Statute and Supervision of Credit Institutions; *Germany*: Section 46(2) of the Law on the Credit System but only through a court order.

[162] *Australia*: Section 11CA(2)(j) of the Banking Act 1959; *Austria*: Article 70(2)1 of the Austrian Banking Act; *Germany*: Section 45(1) of the Law on the Credit System.

[163] *Norway*: Section 32 of the Law on Commercial Banks.

[164] *Luxembourg*: Article 59(2)(b) of the Law on the Financial Sector; *Switzerland*: Article 23ter(1bis) of the Federal Law on Banks and Savings Banks.

[165] *Austria*: Article 20(6)3 of the Austrian Banking Act; *France*: Article 46-1 of Law No. 84-46 on the Activities and Supervision of Credit Institutions.

[166] *France*: Article 46-1 of Law No. 84-46 on the Activities and Supervision of Credit Institutions.

[167] See Chapters IX and X below.

[168] *United States*: 12 U.S.C. § 1821(d)(2)(A); *Netherlands*: Article 72(1) of the Law on Supervision of the Credit System, but only for receivers.

[169] *Austria*: Article 84(2) of the Austrian Banking Act under provisional administration; *Portugal*: Article 143(2)(a) of the Legal Framework of Credit Institutions and Financial Companies, approved by Decree-Law No. 298/92 under provisional administration.

[170] *Netherlands*: Article 28(3)(a) of the Law on Supervision of the Credit System, under provisional administration.

Measures Affecting Bank Operations

This is the category of corrective measures that is most often found in banking law. Typically, the regulator is authorized by law to issue a guideline, direction, or order: to cease and desist from certain banking activities;[171] to take any measure required to cure the bank's condition;[172] to prohibit the bank from engaging in certain operations or to impose other restrictions on its business;[173] or to order the bank to dispose of shareholdings it owns.[174] In some countries, the bank regulator may attach operational restrictions and other conditions to a bank's operating license.[175]

The following provisions of the banking law of *Australia*, reproduced in substance, illustrate the kinds of corrective action that may be ordered by the bank regulator:

(2) The kinds of direction a bank may be given are as follows:

    a) a direction to comply with the whole or a part of prudential regulation or a prudential standard;

    b) a direction to order an audit of the affairs of the bank, at the expense of the bank, by an auditor chosen by the bank regulator;

    c) a direction to do all or any of the following:

        i) remove a director, secretary, executive officer or employee of the bank from office;

        ii) ensure a director, secretary, executive officer or employee of the bank does not take part in the management or

        iii) appoint a person or persons as a director, secretary, executive officer or employee of the bank for such term as the bank regulator directs;

---

[171] *Belgium*: Article 57(1)(2) of the Law on the Statute and Supervision of Credit Institutions; *Canada*: Section 645(1)(a) of the Bank Act; *United States*: 12 U.S.C. § 1818(b)(1).

[172] *France*: Article 43 of Law No. 84-46 on the Activities and Supervision of Credit Institutions; *Netherlands*: Articles 14 and 28(2) of the Law on Supervision of the Credit System; *Switzerland*: Article 23ter(1) of the Federal Law relating to Banks and Savings Banks.

[173] *Australia*: Section 11CA(k)-(n) of the Banking Act 1959; *Austria*: Article 70(2) of the Austrian Banking Act; *France*: Article 45 sub 3 of Law No. 84-46 on the Activities and Supervision of Credit Institutions; *Germany*: Sections 45(1) and 46(1) of the Law on the Credit System.

[174] *Belgium*: Article 57(1)(2) of the Law on the Statute and Supervision of Credit Institutions.

[175] *Australia*: Section 9(4) of the Banking Act 1959; *England*: Section 12(2) of the Banking Act 1987.

d) a direction to remove any auditor of the bank from office and appoint another auditor to hold office for such term as the bank regulator directs;

e) a direction not to give any financial accommodation to any person;

f) a direction not to accept the deposit of any amount;

g) a direction not to borrow any amount;

h) a direction not to accept any payment on account of share capital, except payments in respect of calls that fell due before the direction was given;

i) a direction not to repay any amount paid on shares;

j) a direction not to pay a dividend on any shares;

k) a direction not to repay any money on deposit or advance;

l) a direction not to pay or transfer any amount to any person, or create an obligation (contingent or otherwise) to do so;

m) a direction not to undertake any financial obligation (contingent or otherwise) on behalf of any other person;

n) any other direction as to the way in which the affairs of the bank are to be conducted or not conducted.

A direction under paragraph (l) not to pay any amount does not apply to the payment or transfer of money pursuant to an order of a court or a process of execution.

(2A) Without limiting the generality of subsection (2), a direction referred to in a paragraph of that subsection may:

a) deal with some only of the matters referred to in that paragraph;

b) deal with a particular class or particular classes of those matters; or

c) make different provision with respect to different matters or different classes of matters.

(3) The direction may deal with the time by which, or period during which, it is to be complied with.

(4) The bank has power to comply with the direction despite anything in its constitution or any contract or arrangement to which it is a party.

(5) The direction has effect until the bank regulator revokes it by notice in writing to the bank. The bank regulator may revoke the direction if, at the time of revocation, it considers that the direction is no longer necessary or appropriate.[176]

---

[176] Section 11CA of the Banking Act 1959.

Before issuing such an order, the effects of the order on the bank's obligations should be carefully considered. In particular, the bank regulator must ensure that the entry into force of an order to a bank does not adversely affect payment instructions or securities transfer orders already given by the bank; this to protect payment and securities transfer systems.[177]

3. Appointment of Observers and Inspectors

Many banking laws provide for the bank regulator to become involved in the management of a bank that fails to comply with the banking law or fails to carry out corrective measures ordered by the regulator. This category ranges from passive involvement in the management of the bank through the appointment of an observer or inspector to taking active regulatory control of the bank through one or more administrators or receivers.

Observers and inspectors must be distinguished from provisional administrators and receivers.[178] Observers and inspectors are agents of the bank regulator and owe their duty entirely to the bank regulator. To the bank concerned, they remain outsiders who are not appointed as bank managers but assigned to the bank as supervisors. Provisional administrators, however, even though they are appointed by or upon the request of the bank regulator, become part of the internal governance structure of the bank.[179] Receivers, though outsiders, usually take complete control of the bank, whereas observers and inspectors do not.

---

[177] See Chapter XIII, Section 2, below, for a discussion of the need to protect payment and securities transfer systems.

[178] As this report deals with banks in distress, it will not discuss the appointment of more or less permanent examiners to a bank as a function of the regular bank supervision process.

[179] There are countries where this distinction is not clearly drawn by the law. E.g., in the *Netherlands*, Article 28 (3) of the Law on Supervision of the Credit System authorizes the regulator to notify a bank that its management may exercise its powers only after approval of one or more persons appointed by the regulator and in compliance with their instructions. In form, such appointment comes close to that of an inspector. In substance, however, the appointment means a *de facto* taking over of the management of the bank; therefore, in this report, it is treated as provisional administration.

Observers

Some banking laws authorize the bank regulator to assign an observer to a bank.[180] Observers are investigators whose task is generally limited to surveillance of, and reporting to the bank regulator on, the activities of the bank. Normally, an observer may not intervene in the bank's business and his consent is not required for management and shareholder decisions.[181] The observer attends management and shareholder meetings. He may have to be consulted on some or all important business decisions of the bank.

Because the activities of the observer have no external effects, his appointment need not be publicly announced. This has the advantage of protecting the bank from an adverse market reaction to the appointment. However, under the influence of growing demand for greater transparency, this advantage may eventually disappear.

Inspectors

In some countries, an inspector may be appointed whose main task is to supervise banking activities. The law may require prior authorization of the inspector for all legal acts and decisions of the bank, including decisions of the general meeting of shareholders.[182] Or the law may charge the inspector with prohibiting the bank to engage in activities that would be detrimental to the bank's financial condition.[183]

Often, the banking law fails to attach sanctions to transactions conducted with third parties without the required consent of the inspector. In civil law countries, this omission would usually be cured by the provisions of company law governing external representation of the bank, which would permit the bank to disavow such transactions for lack of authority to conclude them, provided that the restriction on

---

[180] *Australia*: Sections 13A–13B of the Banking Act 1959; *Germany*: Section 46(1) of the Law on the Credit System; *Switzerland*: Article 23quater of the Federal Law relating to Banks and Savings Banks.

[181] In *Germany*, the consent of the inspector may be required for management and shareholder actions, but the failure to obtain such consent has no external legal effect; instead, fines may be imposed in case of noncompliance with the requirement; Reischauer/Kleinhans, *Kreditwesengesetz-Kommentar*, Article 46-para 9.

[182] *Belgium*: Article 57(1)(1) of the Law on the Statute and Supervision of Credit Institutions.

[183] *Argentina*: Article 34 of the Financial Institutions Law; *Austria*: Article 84(2) of the Banking Act.

the powers of the bank's managers had been recorded in the public register of companies before the activity occurred; without such registration, the absence of consent of the inspector could normally not be invoked against counterparties of the bank.

Sometimes, the banking law imposes a two-step procedure, requiring that the appointment of an inspector be preceded by a notice of noncompliance, which may or may not order the bank to take corrective measures; an inspector may then be appointed only if in the opinion of the regulator the bank's response to the notice is inadequate or the bank fails to comply with the order.[184]

The control exercised by an inspector falls short of bank management. The inspector's role is largely a passive one, as he has only the right to give or to withhold his consent and may not initiate acts or decisions. The inspector does not have the power to enforce compliance by the bank with the law or the instructions of the regulator, not even where noncompliance is the principal ground for his appointment. Therefore, if the purpose of the appointment of an inspector is to restore the bank to health, more will be needed than the authority to disallow inappropriate transactions, especially if it concerns a large, modern full-service bank. Restructuring such an institution will require proactive involvement in all departments of the bank—for instance, to cut out waste, to close unprofitable undertakings or excessively leveraged positions, or to improve accounting, auditing, and risk management systems and procedures. It is questionable whether an inspector lacking the right of managerial initiative would be legally permitted or even practically able to leverage his veto powers to such an extent that he could force the bank's management to initiate actions that he is not authorized to initiate himself. Moreover, if that were the legislative intent behind the appointment of an inspector, it would be more efficient for the law directly to grant managerial authority to the inspector.

Another disadvantage of the appointment of an inspector is that, to give the requirement of his consent external legal effect, the bank must be notified of the appointment and the appointment must be made public. This may trigger an adverse market reaction. Moreover, in some jurisdictions, the appointment of an inspector may make the regulator liable for errors committed by the inspector.

---

[184] *Belgium*: Article 57 (1)(1) of the Law on the Statute and Supervision of Credit Institutions.

The principal advantage of appointing an inspector is that it affords the bank regulator a close eye on the bank's operations, providing it with valuable information about the performance of the bank's managers. As such, it may precede the removal of bank managers by the regulator and their replacement with one or more provisional administrators.

VI

Exceptional Financial Support to Insolvent Banks

As treated here, exceptional financial support is provided to a bank only when it is insolvent. It should be distinguished from liquidity support provided to banks by a central bank as lender of last resort.[185]

Typically, exceptional financial support, or "open bank assistance" as it is sometimes called, is provided to a bank in financial distress in order to rescue the bank or to prepare it for a merger with another financial institution, when its failure is judged to have serious consequences for the banking system, for instance, because the bank is too big to fail, or when such assistance is required in the context of a systemic banking crisis. Usually, exceptional financial support is corrective in the sense that it provides remedial assistance aimed at preserving the bank's franchise in one form or another. A fundamental objective of exceptional financial support is that the bank receiving support continues to operate as a legally independent corporation. Therefore, as discussed here, exceptional financial support is provided to the bank in distress and does not include official financial support that is extended to another institution to facilitate a sale, merger, or purchase and assumption transaction whereby the bank is transferred to that institution.[186]

The justification for providing exceptional financial support to insolvent banks must be sought in the systemic consequences of with-

---

[185] See Chapter I, Section 5, above. In theory, exceptional financial support may also be required in cases where a bank is solvent but is unable to meet the collateral requirements for central bank credit; as such cases are relatively rare, they are ignored in this discussion.

[186] See Chapter XI, below, for a discussion of official financial support provided in the context of bank resolution procedures involving transfers of banks in distress.

holding it. Therefore, the decision to provide exceptional financial support will depend on several factors. One is whether household deposits are protected by deposit insurance. In many countries, the monetary authorities will be more inclined to extend financial assistance when there is no deposit insurance than when there is, although, in others, there may be some pressure to provide assistance in order to protect the deposit insurance fund. Another factor is whether failure of the bank would have unacceptable consequences for the banking system as a whole, either because failure of the bank would cause serious difficulties for other banks that are creditors of the failing bank (e.g., because its size or the nature of its operations does not permit an orderly resolution) or because failure of the bank is expected to lead to a dangerous loss of public confidence in the banking system. Large size is not the only criterion. As is illustrated by the small-bank crisis in England in the early 1990s, the failure of a significant number of small banks can endanger the banking system if it is not contained (which it was). Also, the failure of a medium-sized bank can seriously tarnish the international reputation of a major financial center (London or New York). A subsidiary consideration may well be that no other institution can be found that is prepared to take over the bank on reasonable terms. A third factor is the seriousness and permanence of the immediate causes leading to the bank's liquidity shortfall. If the causes are systemic, for instance where they are related to the failure of other financial institutions, the authorities may step in aggressively with liquid resources to combat the spreading of contagion. If, however, the bank is in trouble because its access to the interbank market has been cut by other banks based on its weak financial condition, the authorities may be more reluctant to ride to the rescue. A fourth factor to be considered by the monetary authorities of a country is that a bank failure may adversely affect international transactions using the country's payment and securities transfer systems and the international reputation of its financial markets.

Exceptional financial support to an insolvent bank may take several forms. It may come as a loan from the central bank, the state, the deposit insurance agency, or commercial sources, as a guarantee for loans provided by others, as a bond swap, or as an equity contribution.

Although, normally, the central bank may extend financial assistance only to solvent institutions, the central bank may nevertheless be authorized to grant exceptional short-term funding to an insolvent bank so as to permit the bank to continue to meet its liabilities, sometimes collateralized by assets that normally are not eligible to be used as security for central bank credit. The state treasury may provide financing directly, or through an intermediary such as the central bank. Alternatively, the deposit insurance agency may provide financial assistance, although the funds available to it to engage in large-scale support would often be inadequate, requiring additional funding from the state treasury.[187] Or the monetary authorities may try to organize funding from commercial sources; however, due to the weak financial condition of the bank, such support will generally not be available without considerable pressure from the authorities or at least their implicit debt-service guarantee.[188]

Bond swaps can be used to exchange central bank or state treasury bonds for nonperforming loans of a bank in distress. Removing nonperforming loan assets from a bank's balance sheet in exchange for central bank or government securities not only strengthens the bank's financial condition, but also frees the bank from the administrative burden of debt collection and thereby helps the bank to focus on the rehabilitation of its core activities. The nonperforming loans may be transferred to a state agency, such as the deposit insurance agency or an asset management corporation, for collection or for a loan workout. In recent years, the bond swap has been among the most frequently used methods in bank restructuring packages.[189]

Special financial assistance may also come in the form of an equity participation by the state in the bank, either directly or indirectly through a financial intermediary that may have been established specifically for that purpose;[190] such equity stakes are often preferred shares in the bank's capital in amounts and on terms that give the state or its agent effective control of the bank and that sufficiently dilute the value of existing equity capital. In some countries, the law authorizes the deposit insurance agency to provide equity funding or an equity funding guarantee.[191] If restructuring of the bank is successful, the

---

[187] E.g., *Norway*: Section 2–12(1) of the Law on Guarantee Schemes for Banks of 1996; *United States*: 12 U.S.C. § 1823(c).

[188] To that end, the deposit insurance agency may be authorized by law to extend guarantees. See, e.g., *Norway*: Section 2–12(1)(b) of the Law on Guarantee Schemes for Banks of 1996; *United States*: 12 U.S.C. § 1823(c)(2)(A)(iii), but only to facilitate the merger or consolidation of the bank with, the sale of assets of the bank to, or the assumption of liabilities or the acquisition of control of the bank by, another institution.

[189] Claudia Dziobek, and Ceyla Pazarbaşioğlu, "Lessons from Systemic Bank Restructuring: A Survey of 24 Countries," IMF Working Paper 97/171 (Washington: International Monetary Fund), 1997, at pp. 15–16.

[190] An example of such intermediary is the Reconstruction Finance Corporation of the *United States,* which between 1933 and 1953 provided equity capital to many banks in distress.

[191] *Norway*: Section 2–12(1)(c) of the Law on Guarantee Schemes for Banks of 1996.

shares may be bought back by the bank or be converted into common stock and sold by the state to the public. An alternative to equity participations may be to provide credit financing in the form of quasi-equity where the ranking of the bank debt so created is contractually subordinated to all other debt of the bank.[192]

The law may require that several conditions must be met before public funding can be deemed justified. These may include that the bank receiving the loan must be threatened with the inability to pay its debts as they become due if the funds are not provided, that the loan is intended to lessen the effects of a systemic banking crisis, that the loan represents the least-cost solution for the regulatory agencies to the bank's problems, and that the bank's management has been competent and has complied with applicable law and regulations.[193] The requirement that open bank assistance, when compared with other bank resolution strategies, represents the least-cost solution means generally that it represents the least financial cost to the fiscal authorities. However, that solution need not be the optimal alternative when viewed from the perspective of the banking system. The solution that carries the least financial cost is not necessarily the solution with the lowest economic cost. Therefore, the law should provide for a safety valve permitting open bank assistance in cases where rescuing the bank is mandated by systemic considerations; the use of this exception may be limited and public accountability may be enhanced by prescribing a restrictive decision-making process involving a broad spectrum of the political establishment.[194]

An important objective in providing exceptional financial support to an insolvent bank is to ensure that, to the extent possible, the full costs of such support are borne by the bank's owners. In principle, special financial support should be provided on terms and conditions that reflect market cost. In practice, however, such terms might not be ascertainable as no financing from market sources would be available for an insolvent bank at any price, whereas financing, if it would be offered on such terms, would be too onerous to fit a restructuring plan.

---

[192] See Gillian Garcia, "Deposit Insurance and Crisis Management," IMF Working Paper 00/57 (Washington: International Monetary Fund), 2000, at pp. 51–52.

[193] *United States*: 12 U.S.C. § 1823(c).

[194] See for this approach the *United States*: 12 U.S.C. § 1823(c)(4)(G) requiring a decision of the Secretary of the Treasury (in consultation with the U.S. President) pursuant to a written recommendation adopted by a two-thirds majority of both the Board of Directors of the FDIC and the Board of Governors of the Federal Reserve System, for the adoption of a bank resolution strategy other than the least-cost solution.

Consequently, special financial support to an insolvent bank may have to be priced at subsidized levels; the difference between those terms and what is assumed to be a fair market price should be charged to the bank's owners.

More generally, the law should require that managers and owners of an insolvent bank suffer consequences of their failure to keep their bank safe and sound. Charging the costs of a bank's failure to the bank's owners, by suspending dividend payments or diluting their equity stake or imposing civil or criminal penalties, precludes the owners from benefiting from official assistance (free ridership) and tends to reduce the moral hazard that a rescue operation poses with respect to other banks. Bank managers guilty of negligence or worse should be removed and made to pay penalties in case of gross negligence or willful misconduct. However, imposing such sanctions on bank owners and managers would not be appropriate in cases where bank failures occur as a result of circumstances beyond their control, such as war or natural disaster. Otherwise, the provision of such disincentives for managers and owners has been identified as a key element of best practices in bank restructuring.[195]

---

[195] Dziobek, and Pazarbaşioğlu, "Lessons from Systemic Bank Restructuring," at p. 15. See also Garcia, "Deposit Insurance and Crisis Management," at p. 51.

VII

Special Moratorium on Debt Service by Banks Under the Banking Law

1. General Observations

Usually, regulatory corrective action cannot be kept secret. When it becomes public knowledge, it may trigger a run on the bank in distress. To reduce the risk that liquidity problems of a bank would balloon into a run on the bank, which could set off runs on other banks, and to buy the bank and the regulators some time to find a solution for the bank's problems, the banking law of some countries authorizes that a temporary and special payment moratorium for some or all of the bank's debt be imposed on creditors of a bank in distress.[196] These moratoria are special in that they differ from the more common and general moratoria that usually accompany a general insolvency proceeding or a bank receivership.

Debt-service moratoria for the benefit of banks in distress are usually justified by considerations at two levels. At the systemic level, a debt-service moratorium for a bank helps stave off a run on the bank and thereby limits the risk that such a run could lead to a general deterioration of trust in the banking system, precipitating a banking crisis. This means, *inter alia,* that the moratorium is carefully managed so as to avoid that the implicit weakness of the bank protected by the moratorium be misinterpreted by the public as a sign of more widespread banking problems. At the commercial level, a debt-service moratorium is intended to be used by the bank and the regulator to improve its condition for the benefit of its creditors or to find a suitable takeover partner.

---

[196] A moratorium covering only part of a bank's obligations may raise difficult questions of equity between creditors whose claims are suspended under the moratorium and creditors whose claims continue to be serviced by the bank.

Whatever its justification, a debt-service moratorium is at the expense of the bank's creditors whose rights are suspended, and is at their risk that, instead of improving, the bank's financial condition will further deteriorate. Therefore, a moratorium should be declared only if it is justified by systemic considerations[197] or if there is a reasonable expectation that the moratorium can and will further the creditors' interests. In order to ensure that the moratorium is used to achieve its objective and that it does not serve to shield unsafe or unsound banking practices, the law may require for a moratorium that the bank be placed under provisional administration and that the moratorium subject to strict time limits. Preferably, a moratorium should be carried out in accordance with a comprehensive corrective action plan adopted by agreement between the bank regulator and the bank.

Nevertheless, where the objective of the moratorium granted to a bank is to rehabilitate the bank while it continues its operations, or where such rehabilitation requires support from the financial markets in the form of equity capital or credit, a special debt moratorium may present a paradox.

First, it is difficult to see how a bank under a moratorium could continue its operations which is a condition for its rehabilitation: ordinary banking services would normally include incurring new liabilities whose payment would be suspended by the moratorium, unless an exception would be made for new obligations of the bank. Assume that such an exception would be made and that only preexisting liabilities would be covered by the moratorium. Assume further that the bank would continue to transact most of its business with the same clients as before the moratorium. Then, the curious situation would develop where most clients of the bank would have two kinds of claims on the bank: old claims on which debt-service payments by the bank would be suspended by the moratorium and new claims on which debt-service payments would not be suspended. Would there be many clients willing to extend new credit to a bank before payments due on their existing credit would be current?

Second, a moratorium would usually be interpreted as a sign of financial weakness and diminish a bank's prospects of meeting its funding needs from the markets at a reasonable cost.[198] Here, the

---

[197] This implies that the authorities would do whatever it takes to make the moratorium a success.

[198] In *Italy*, it should help that the law specifies that a moratorium does not constitute a state of insolvency—Article 74(3) of the Law of 1993 on Matters Concerning Banking and Credit.

paradox is that, while the objective of the moratorium is to protect the bank from its creditors, and thereby to keep the bank alive and to enable it to return to viability, the moratorium tends to deny the bank the market funding that it needs to become viable again. Therefore, the more banks rely on financial markets for their funding and the sale of their services, the less effective special moratoria for banks will be, except to gain time needed to engineer a sale or merger of the bank.

These concerns are addressed by the provisions of the banking law of *Switzerland* that govern the special moratorium for banks that encounter liquidity problems but are not overindebted.[199] By limiting the moratorium to cases where the bank concerned is not overindebted, the risk of granting preferential treatment to new creditors over existing creditors is reduced. In contrast, this risk is significantly greater under an otherwise similar provisional administration with moratorium permitted by the banking law of *Austria*, because it applies especially to banks that are overindebted or insolvent, even though the provisional administration and therefore the moratorium will be granted only if the overindebtedness or insolvency is likely to be cured.[200] The banking law of *Switzerland* contains the following additional safeguards:

1. During the moratorium, the bank continues to do business under the supervision and in accordance with the instructions of the administrator; it may not, however, perform legal acts which would prejudice the legitimate interests of creditors or would favor individual creditors at the expense of others. Payments to creditors may be made only with the consent of the administrator. He is authorized to order, at his discretion, payments to creditors with claims that are due and payable up to a specific ceiling; in doing so, it shall be necessary to take proper account of the interests of creditors with claims protected by preferences established by contract or law as well as the interests of small creditors. Such payments may not exceed one half of the amounts for which, according to the administrator's assessment of the estate, coverage is available.

2. During the moratorium, the court may at any time take such additional measures as the circumstances dictate and serve the interests of the bank or the creditors. In particular, the court may require that, to be valid, the conclusion of new transactions, the transfer

---

[199] Articles 29–35 of the Federal Law on Banks and Savings Banks.
[200] *Austria*: Article 83(1) of the Austrian Banking Act.

of real estate, the establishment of liens, or the granting of guarantees shall require the consent of the administrator; such requirements must be published.[201]

This Swiss moratorium is instituted and supervised by the courts. Such *judicial moratoria* should be distinguished from *extrajudicial moratoria,* which are instituted and supervised by another authority such as the government or the bank regulator.

2. Judicial Moratoria

Several countries offer a debt-service moratorium that is instituted by court order and supervised by the court, at the request of the bank concerned,[202] at the request of the bank regulator,[203] or at the request of a court-appointed administrator.[204]

Alternatively, the law may *ipso facto* attach a moratorium to the appointment of a provisional administrator by the court.[205]

The grounds on which a judicial moratorium may be ordered differ from country to country.

In *Switzerland*, the law provides for three different moratoria that may apply to banks.[206] These are a judicial moratorium under the banking law designed to provide some breathing room for the benefit of a bank that is illiquid but not overindebted;[207] a judicial moratorium for banks that may be overindebted, as part of a composition procedure under the general insolvency law that applies to banks;[208] and

---

[201] Articles 32(2) and (3) of the Federal Law on Banks and Savings Banks. Cf., *Austria*: Article 86 of the Austrian Banking Act.

[202] *Luxembourg*: Article 60(2) of the Law of 1993 on the Financial Sector; *Switzerland*: Article 29(1) of the Federal Law on Banks and Savings Banks.

[203] *Luxembourg*: Article 60(2) of the Law of 1993 on the Financial Sector.

[204] *France*: Article 36 of Law No. 84-148 on the Prevention and Amicable Settlement of Difficulties of Enterprises.

[205] *Austria*: Article 86 of the Austrian Banking Act.

[206] See for a comparative analysis of these moratoria: Peter Merz, and Marc Raggenbass, "Switzerland," in *International Bank Insolvencies: A Central Bank's Perspective*," ed. by Mario Giovanoli and Gregor Heinrich (The Hague: Kluwer Law International), 1999, at pp. 221–223; and Eva H.G. Hüpkes, *The Legal Aspects of Bank Insolvency* (The Hague: Kluwer Law International), 2000, at pp. 70–74.

[207] Articles 29(1) and (2) of the Federal Law on Banks and Savings Banks.

[208] Articles 293 ff. of the Debt Enforcement and Bankruptcy Law, and Article 37 of the Federal Law on Banks and Savings Banks.

a rarely used extrajudicial moratorium providing for the rescheduling of debt of otherwise sound banks that face a liquidity crisis.[209]

In *Luxembourg*, a moratorium may be granted:

> ...if the creditworthiness of the institution in question is impaired or if it is experiencing liquidity difficulties, whether or not it has ceased payments; if there is a danger that the institution will not be able to fulfill its obligations completely; or

> if the authorization of the institution has been withdrawn but the relevant decision is not yet final.[210]

Generally, the law does not explicitly require for a debt-service moratorium to a bank that the moratorium be justified either by systemic considerations or by a reasonable expectation that the bank's difficulties will be corrected.[211] Such requirement may be implicit in a statutory provision that the moratorium be terminated if it appears that the moratorium will not cure the bank's financial difficulties,[212] or where it becomes evident during the moratorium that the bank has become insolvent.[213]

In order to mitigate the risk that, under cover of the moratorium, the bank would engage in unsafe or unsound banking activities that would worsen its condition, the law sometimes requires the written authorization of the bank's supervisory auditors for all acts and decisions of the bank,[214] or provides for the appointment of a provisional administrator from the time that the petition for a moratorium is filed with the court.[215]

3. Extrajudicial Moratoria

Extrajudicial moratoria are characterized by the fact that they do not require a court order for their institution and that they are not subject

---

[209] Articles 25 ff. of the Federal Law on Banks and Savings Banks.

[210] Article 60(1) of the Law of 1993 on the Financial Sector.

[211] Note that in *Austria*, Article 83(1) of the Austrian Banking Act permits banks to apply for provisional administration, and the accompanying debt-service moratorium, only if their overindebtedness or insolvency is likely to be cured.

[212] *Luxembourg*: Article 61(1)(a) of the Law of 1993 on the Financial Sector.

[213] *Switzerland*: Article 35(2) of the Federal Law on Banks and Savings Banks. However, such a condition is specified by the law for granting an exceptional six-month extension of an existing moratorium—Article 35(1).

[214] *Luxembourg*: Article 60(13) of the Law of 1993 on the Financial Sector.

[215] *Luxembourg*: Article 60(12) of the Law of 1993 on the Financial Sector; *Switzerland*: Articles 29(1)bis and 30(1) of the Federal Law on Banks and Savings Banks.

to court supervision. The moratorium may be declared by the bank regulator,[216] or by the provisional administrator with the approval of the bank regulator.[217] Not all countries where the moratorium is authorized require that the moratorium be administered by a provisional administrator or receiver.[218]

The grounds on which an extrajudicial moratorium may be declared vary. Some laws specifically refer to the need to protect the interests of bank depositors[219] or bank creditors in general.[220] The law may prescribe that the moratorium is mandated by exceptional circumstances[221] or that the moratorium is needed to stave off bankruptcy.[222]

Sometimes the law provides for two different kinds of special moratoria, one for incidental banking problems and one to prevent or to resolve systemic banking crises. This is the case in *Germany* where the banking law both empowers the bank regulator to grant a moratorium in response to incidental banking problems[223] and authorizes the federal government by regulation to establish a special moratorium for any bank when a banking crisis threatens, namely, if there is reason to fear that banks may encounter financial difficulties that warrant expectations of grave danger to the national economy and particularly to the orderly functioning of general payments.[224]

During the moratorium, the law may permit the bank to complete transactions in progress and to enter into new transactions needed to complete transactions in progress.[225] As is usually the case for court-administered moratoria, the law may provide that no execution,

---

[216] *Denmark*: Article 46(1) of the Consolidated Law on Commercial Banks and Savings Banks; *Germany*: Article 46a(1)1 of the Law on the Credit System.

[217] *Italy*: Article 74(1) of the Law of 1993 on Matters Concerning Banking and Credit.

[218] No provisional administrator or receiver is required in *Denmark* or *Germany*, or for the rescheduling of debt-service payments in *Switzerland*.

[219] *Denmark*: Section 46 of the Law on Commercial Banks and Savings Banks.

[220] *Germany*: Article 46a(1) *juncto* Article 46(1) of the Law on the Credit System; *Italy*: Article 74 of the Law of 1993 on Matters Concerning Banking and Credit.

[221] *Italy: Ibid.*

[222] *Germany*: Section 46a(1) of the Law on the Credit System.

[223] *Germany*: Section 46a(1)1 of the Law on the Credit System.

[224] *Germany*: Section 47(1) of the Law on the Credit System.

[225] *Germany*: Section 46a(1) of the Law on the Credit System, but only if and to the extent that the deposit guarantee agency provides the funds required for the purpose or undertakes to compensate the bank for any reduction in asset values resulting from these transactions required for the full compensation of the bank's creditors. The regulator may authorize exceptions to the moratorium as required for the administration of the bank; Section 46a(1).

attachment, or foreclosure can be carried out or completed concerning bank assets protected by the moratorium.[226]

In *Switzerland*, the extrajudicial moratorium is instituted by the government and is limited to a rescheduling of repayments on bank debt if the bank is exposed to continuing and excessive withdrawals, and then only if it is established by a special audit report that the affected claims are fully covered and that during the postponement payments of interest can be maintained.[227]

4. Entry into Force and Termination of Moratoria

The time at which a debt-service moratorium for a bank enters into force is of crucial importance to net settlement systems for payments and securities transfers. Often, when a moratorium is granted, payment orders issued by the bank are being processed by a net settlement system at home or abroad without knowledge of the moratorium. Following the traditional rule that gives effect to the moratorium at the beginning of the day on which it is granted may require the clearinghouses concerned to reverse their transactions for that day, which could cause them to suspend operations until the administrative backlog has been cleared; this could create considerable systemic risks for the economies of the countries concerned and the international monetary system as a whole. The issue is discussed more fully below.[228]

A debt-service moratorium for a bank should terminate when it is no longer needed because its objectives have been achieved,[229] or when there is no longer a reasonable expectation that the bank will avoid insolvency.[230] In addition, the law may limit the duration of

---

[226] *Germany*: Section 46a(1) of the Law on the Credit System; *Italy*: Article 74(2) of the Law of 1993 on Matters Concerning Banking and Credit.

[227] Articles 25 ff. of the Federal Law on Banks and Savings Banks. This instrument has not been used in Switzerland since the 1930s; it may nevertheless be a useful tool to combat systemic liquidity crises—Merz and Raggenbass, "Switzerland," at p. 221.

[228] See the discussion of effects of the opening of insolvency proceedings on payment systems in Chapter XIII, Section 2, below.

[229] *Austria*: Article 90(2)1 of the Austrian Banking Act; *Switzerland*: Article 33(2) of the Federal Law on Banks and Savings Banks.

[230] *Luxembourg*: Article 60(1) of the Law of 1993 on the Financial Sector; *Switzerland*: Article 35(2) of the Federal Law on Banks and Savings Banks.

the moratorium to an overall time limit, which may be subject to extension.[231]

If the moratorium is terminated because bank restructuring is deemed to fail, the bank should be closed and be turned over to a regulatory bank receiver or to the bankruptcy court.[232]

---

[231] *Austria*: one year with extension upon request by the bank regulator with the consent of the Minister of Justice—Article 90(2)2 of the Austrian Banking Act; *Italy*: up to one month with extension up to a further two months—Article 74(1) of the Law of 1993 on Matters Concerning Banking and Credit; *Luxembourg*: six months without extension—Article 60(8) of the Law of 1993 on the Financial Sector. In *Switzerland*, as a rule, moratoria are granted for one year with the possibility of one extension of another year—Article 29(2) of the Federal Law on Banks and Savings Banks; pursuant to Article 35(1) of that law, an exceptional extension of six months is permitted "if it becomes apparent during the moratorium that the bank can achieve an extrajudicial rehabilitation."

[232] E.g., *Denmark*: Article 47 of the Law on Commercial Banks and Savings Banks; *Switzerland*: Article 35(2) of the Federal Law on Banks and Savings Banks.

Principal Objectives To Be Pursued by Law

The law should prescribe a graduated corrective response to non-compliance with prudential requirements only where the levels of noncompliance can be hierarchically ranked; otherwise, the extent of corrective action should be controlled by the need to achieve success tempered by administrative law principles, such as the principle of proportionality.

The authority for taking corrective action should be clearly circumscribed by law. Statutory grounds for taking corrective action should grant the bank regulator sufficient discretion to counter unforeseen conditions with a prompt and adequate regulatory response; in particular, such grounds should not be so narrowly prescribed that they would preclude proper or timely corrective action.

Where the bank regulator has identified a significant deficiency in compliance by a bank with prudential requirements, the banking law should require that, whenever in the judgment of the bank regulator conditions permit, the bank submit to the bank regulator for its acceptance a plan consisting of one or more specific corrective measures to be executed by the bank in order to correct that deficiency.

The law should require that exceptional financial support to rescue the business of an otherwise failing bank should be provided only when justified by systemic considerations, and that, to the extent possible, the costs of bank rescue operations should be borne by the banks' owners, even where this means depriving them of their economic interest in the banks.

A debt-service moratorium should be granted to a bank only if it is justified by systemic considerations or if there is a reasonable expectation that the bank's difficulties will be corrected. It should be carried out in accordance with a comprehensive corrective action plan. Granting a debt-service moratorium to a bank may adversely affect its position in the financial markets and therefore its ability to obtain funding at costs that are compatible with its restructuring plan. Therefore, in assessing the likelihood that the bank's difficulties will be corrected, the financial market effects of the moratorium should be taken into account.

VIII

Taking Control of a Bank Under the Banking Law: Common Issues

1. Survey of Procedures

In most countries, the corrective measures described in the foregoing must be administered to a bank within its existing governance structure. Bank owners retain their rights and bank managers remain in place. However, preserving the corporate structure of a bank imposes limitations on the scope of corrective measures that can be taken without the cooperation of the decision-making organs of the bank. If management or owners do not cooperate with the bank regulator in restructuring their bank, or if they are judged unable to do so, the bank regulator must use stronger medicine and take control of the bank, either directly or through a provisional administrator or receiver.

A comparative analysis of national banking laws produces two general categories of procedures for taking control of a bank in distress, namely:

(a) Bank administration procedures set forth in the banking law. These are discussed in this section of the book; they consist of either:

- a regime of regulatory administration in which the regulator, either directly or through a provisional administrator or receiver, takes control of a bank without judicial involvement; or

- a regime of judicial administration, in which control of the bank is taken by a provisional administrator or receiver appointed and supervised by the court, usually in cooperation with the bank regulator; and

(b) Judicial insolvency procedures governed by a general or special insolvency law and carried out under judicial administration. In addition to a formal bankruptcy regime, the law may contain an

103

extensive rehabilitation procedure offering a combination of provisional administration and receivership.[233] In countries where the general insolvency law applies to banks, it is common for the law to include special provisions for banks, recognizing their unique position, the role of the bank regulator, and the public interest in a safe and sound banking system; for example, the law may involve the bank regulator in the judicial ruling on a petition for opening insolvency proceedings against a bank.[234]

In some countries, the law subjects banks to both bank administration procedures under the banking law, and judicial insolvency procedures under the general insolvency law (*Australia, Austria, Denmark, France, Netherlands, Switzerland*) or under a special insolvency law for financial institutions (*Canada*).[235] In a second group of countries, banks are excluded from judicial insolvency procedures and may be submitted only to regulatory bank administration under the banking law (*Italy, Norway, United States*) or judicial administration under the banking law (*Luxembourg*). In a third group of countries, judicial insolvency procedures do apply to banks, to the exclusion of bank administration procedures (*Belgium, England, Germany*).

Taking control of a bank under bank administration procedures in the banking law, regardless of whether this is done under regulatory administration or under judicial administration, serves one of two immediate objectives, namely: to save the bank as a going concern, or to close the bank.

- Saving a bank as a going concern, as the term is used in this book, is a broad and complex concept covering several kinds of arrangement that ensure that the bank's core business continues in operation, within the bank's preserved corporate structure or as a new corporation or as part of another corporation. Thus, it may involve providing open-bank assistance and managing and operating the bank back to compliance with prudential regulations either through

---

[233] Examples are found in *England*: Part II of the Insolvency Act 1986, which is made applicable to banks by the Banks (Administration Proceedings) Order 1989; and *France*: Law No. 84-148 on the Prevention and Amicable Resolution of Difficulties of Enterprises, and Law No. 85-98 on the Judicial Rehabilitation and Liquidation of Enterprises that apply to banks.

[234] Judicial insolvency procedures are discussed in Chapter XIII, below.

[235] In *Canada*, banks and federally regulated trust and insurance companies are subject to a special insolvency law, the Winding-up and Restructuring Act. General federal insolvency law does not apply to banks; Duffy, "Canada," at p. 36.

a provisional administrator who takes control of the bank's management, or through a receiver who usually assumes the powers of all organs of the bank including its owners. Saving the bank as a going concern need not preserve the rights of its owners in the bank's business. In some cases, it may require the forced purchase of the bank's outstanding shares from existing owners and the sale of the shares to new owners. In others, it may require the transfer of all or substantially all of the bank's business, for instance through a purchase and assumption transaction, to another financial institution, moving the bank's business out of the bank's corporation and leaving the bank's former owners with an empty corporate shell. Obviously, it is possible that only part of the bank's business is saved and that the remainder is liquidated.

- Closing a bank usually is done in a receivership and consists of the liquidation of at least the bank's core banking activities and revocation of its banking license.

Like all bank regulation, taking control of a bank serves the general purpose of maintaining a safe and sound banking system and reducing the systemic risks of a bank failure. Just as taking control of a bank serves a systemic purpose, the choice between saving a bank as a going concern and closing a bank should also be made on the basis of systemic considerations. In general, this means that the authorities should be prepared to save a bank as a going concern only if its failure would have significant systemic consequences. This systemic objective should be weighed against the interests of the bank's creditors, including the deposit insurance agency: generally, bank creditors may expect to be paid as much as they would receive in a traditional liquidation of the bank. In the absence of sufficient systemic justification, banks should be allowed to fail, just like other enterprises.

Taking control of a bank is intrusive and restricts or eliminates the right of the bank's owners to exercise control over the bank's management. Under regulatory administration, the protection of creditor rights is generally inadequate, even though creditors may be able to appeal decisions of the regulator or administrator to the courts. This raises the issue of *ex ante* judicial involvement. In some countries, provisional administration and receivership are deemed so invasive and their effects on shareholder and creditor rights are considered so serious that the law subjects them to judicial administration.[236] With

---

[236] See Section 4, below, for a discussion of the advantages and disadvantages of judicial administration and the *ex ante* review that it offers.

respect to other forms of corrective action the issue hardly arises, and judicial involvement usually does not extend beyond the normal administrative or civil appeals process.

2. Bank Administration Procedures

In most of the countries reviewed, bank administration is carried out by a provisional administrator or a receiver appointed by the bank regulator or by the courts. In some countries, however, the bank regulator may take control of a bank directly.

Taking Direct Control of a Bank

In *Australia*, at the option of the regulator, provisional administration may be carried out by taking control of the business of a bank either directly by the regulator or through an administrator appointed by the regulator.[237] In *Canada*, the regulator may impose provisional administration on a bank by taking direct control of the assets of the bank and the assets under its administration, or by taking control of the bank;[238] although Canadian law does not provide for the appointment of a provisional administrator, one or more persons may be appointed by the regulator to assist the regulator in the management of the bank.[239] In the *United States*, the FDIC may be appointed or appoint itself as conservator or receiver of an insured bank.[240]

Compared with the appointment of a provisional administrator or a receiver, taking direct control of a bank has distinct advantages. These are chiefly that taking direct control saves time by avoiding an appointment process and avoids the inherent risk of leaks that would tip off the financial markets or bank managers or owners. Taking direct control of a bank allows the regulator to address adequately emergency situations requiring immediate intervention, albeit as a temporary measure; after the bank and its assets have been secured, the regulator may transfer control of the bank to an administrator or receiver. Taking direct control of a bank also has costs, however. The principal disad-

---

[237] Section 13A(1) of the Banking Act 1959.

[238] Section 648(1) of the Bank Act; the section also provides that this power may not be exercised if the Minister of Finance (who presides over, and is responsible for, the office of the bank regulator) advises the regulator that the minister is of the opinion that it is not in the public interest to do so.

[239] Section 649(3) of the Bank Act.

[240] 12 U.S.C. § 1821(c)(2)–(4).

vantages of direct regulatory control of a bank are that bank regulators are usually not well qualified to manage a bank, and that maintaining an arm's-length relation to the bank through an independent outsider serving as administrator or receiver permits the regulator to avoid the appearance of a conflict between its responsibilities as bank supervisor and its trustee-like duties as administrator or receiver, especially if there had been deficiencies in supervision.

In the countries where the bank regulator may take direct control of a bank, its powers are generally the same as those of a provisional administrator or receiver. Therefore, and to keep the following discussion simple, the case where the bank regulator may take direct control of a bank or of its business or assets shall generally be subsumed under the appointment of a provisional administrator or a receiver.

Appointment of an Administrator Or Receiver

Bank administration procedures can be distinguished according to their principal objective:

- Provisional administration consists of the appointment of one or more provisional administrators who take over the management of the bank, with the goal of managing the bank back to compliance with prudential requirements, or to preserve the value of the bank while it is being prepared for transfer to another institution in a sale or merger, or for liquidation.

  In many of the countries where it is offered, provisional administration is a form of regulatory administration (*Australia, Canada, Italy, France, Netherlands, United States*): provisional administrators are appointed by the bank regulator and their activities are not subject to judicial supervision. There are countries, however, where provisional administration is judicial in nature as it is instituted and supervised by the court (*Austria, Luxembourg, Switzerland*).

  In countries where the general insolvency law applies to banks, it may include rehabilitation procedures that provide for a judicial form of provisional administration.[241]

---

[241] See for judicial provisional administration, *England*: Section 8 of the Insolvency Act 1987; *France*: the rehabilitation provisions of Law No. 85-98 on the Judicial Rehabilitation and Liquidation of Enterprises, and Articles 34–36 of Law No. 84-148 on the Prevention and Amicable Resolution of Difficulties of Enterprises.

- Receivership consists of the appointment of a receiver who takes full control of the bank, in order to restructure the bank, pending its transfer to another institution in a sale or merger, or to close and liquidate the bank. The objective is to minimize systemic effects of the bank's failure while maximizing the value of the bank for its creditors. This may be done by preserving those parts of the bank's business whose continued operation is important for the banking system, or to liquidate the bank insofar as its continued operation is not needed.

In several countries, receivership may be carried out under regulatory administration (*France, Denmark, Italy, Norway, Spain, United States*). In others, it is subject to judicial administration (*Luxembourg, Netherlands*).

In several countries (*Canada, France, Italy, Luxembourg, Netherlands, United States*), the banking law offers both procedures for banks. In others, the banking law offers only provisional administration (*Australia, Austria, Portugal, Switzerland*) or only receivership (*Denmark, Norway*).

3. Issues Common to Bank Administration Procedures

The following issues are common to bank administration procedures.

Role of the Deposit Insurance Agency

In some countries, the law provides for the appointment of the deposit insurance agency as provisional administrator or receiver.[242] The appointment of the deposit insurance agency as administrator for a bank is problematic, because it is likely to create a conflict of interest between the agency's duties as a trustee and its own interests as a major creditor of the bank following its subrogation to the rights of depositors after payment by the agency on their deposit claims. The conflict may appear when the deposit insurance agency is presented with a choice between its own short-term financial interests and the long-term interests of the banking system. For instance, there may be situations in which the deposit insurance agency would prefer a certain bank resolution strategy because it carries a lower financial cost than

---

[242] *United States*: 12 U.S.C. §§ 191 and 203(a).

another strategy, even though the latter would produce a significantly stronger banking system whose long-term advantages must be expected to outweigh the difference in current financial outlays.

Also, permitting the deposit insurance agency to take control of a bank may be to the disadvantage of other bank creditors: as a major creditor, the deposit insurance agency would not be expected to offer other creditors the same impartial treatment in the verification or negotiated settlement of their claims as they would receive from an independent judiciary. This would tend to decrease the trust of the general public in the bank resolution system. And, as a practical matter, it would prompt bank creditors to appeal decisions of the administrator in the courts more frequently than otherwise.

Selection of Administrators and Receivers

In most countries, the law provides that provisional administrators and receivers of banks are selected by the bank regulator, even when they are appointed by another authority.

As a rule, provisional administrators and receivers are selected from outside the staff of the bank regulator. There are exceptions, however: in one country, the law expressly permits the bank regulator to appoint one of its own officials to assume the temporary management of a bank,[243] while in others the bank regulator may itself take control of a bank.[244]

Notification and Publicity

To bind the bank, it must be notified of the appointment of a provisional administrator or receiver. To have the desired external legal effect of binding counterparties of the bank, the appointment must be announced to the general public, for instance, in a newspaper of general circulation or in the Official Gazette of the country, or by entering the appointment in the public register of companies or banks. Although the announcement of the appointment of a provisional administrator or a receiver for a troubled bank may have a calming effect on the public, especially if the bank experiences liquidity problems, there is a risk that the appointment and its public announce-

---

[243] *Italy*: Article 76(1) of the Law of 1993 on Matters Concerning Banking and Credit.
[244] *Australia*: Section 13A(1) of the Banking Act 1959; *Canada*: Section 648(1) of the Bank Act.

ment would precipitate a run on the bank and worsen the bank's condition. This risk can be reduced by combining the appointment of a provisional administrator or receiver with a properly structured special moratorium on debt-service payments by the bank.

Plans of Action

As noted for corrective action, a plan of action will greatly contribute to successful regulatory intervention. After an assessment of the bank's financial condition, the provisional administrator or receiver would prepare and present to the bank regulator or the court a report analyzing the available options. These options would mainly include the restructuring of the bank, transfer of the bank in whole or in part on a going concern basis to another institution in a sale or merger, and closure through liquidation of the bank. The analysis would include for each of the options, a comparative assessment of the probability of success, a cost-benefit calculation, and an estimate of the time required for its execution. The report will need to be discussed with the government if it includes assistance from the state budget.

Thereafter, the bank regulator or the court should decide on a plan of action for the bank, including a business plan, describing the measures to be taken, setting standards by which progress in the plan's execution is to be measured, and specifying a time period for achieving the goals of the plan. Based on the plan, the bank regulator may impose restrictions on some or all of the bank's activities.

Preferably, such action plans are established by the bank regulator in close consultation, or better yet in agreement, with the administrator or receiver, with the government to the extent that state funding is required, and also with the bank's management and owners insofar as these retain authority, in order to ensure "ownership" of the plan by all parties concerned and to reduce uncertainties concerning the objectives of the provisional administration or receivership and the means to achieve them.

Concurrence of Regulatory and Judicial Administration

In countries where during a provisional administration or receivership instituted by the bank regulator another administrator or receiver can be appointed by the courts, or *vice versa*, questions may arise as to the competing powers of these officials.

In *France*, when a provisional administrator has been appointed under Article 44 of the Banking Law (Law No. 84-46), the powers of a judicial administrator appointed under the General Insolvency Law (Law No. 85–98) are limited to supervision of the bank's operations.[245] In *Australia*, the law provides that the appointment of a provisional administrator by the bank regulator terminates the appointment of an externally appointed liquidator, receiver, or other administrator, and that while a provisional administrator is in control of a bank's business such external appointment must not be made without the approval of the bank regulator.[246]

In *Canada*, an order of the Governor in Council vesting the shares of a bank in the deposit insurance corporation constitutes the latter as the *exclusive* receiver of the assets and undertaking of the bank or of such part thereof as may be specified in the order,[247] until the bank is turned over to the courts for liquidation under the Winding-up and Restructuring Act.

4. Regulatory Administration Versus Judicial Administration

This subsection offers a brief discussion of some comparative advantages and disadvantages of regulatory administration and judicial administration in taking control of banks. The discussion will focus on receivership. Provisional administration is not explicitly covered because, in several countries, it is not instituted and carried out under judicial administration, although many of the arguments advanced may apply where it is. Judicial insolvency procedures are implicitly included in the discussion, as the choice to make banks subject to judicial insolvency procedures in lieu of a special receivership procedure under the banking law will in part be driven by considerations concerning judicial administration.

In several countries, banks may be submitted to a judicial receivership under the banking law or the insolvency law or both (*Australia, Austria, Belgium, Canada, Denmark, England, France, Germany,*

---

[245] Article 46-4 of Law No. 84-46 on the Activities and Supervision of Credit Institutions.

[246] Section 15A(1) and (2) of the Banking Act 1959. The external appointment referred to could be made, e.g., under company law or general insolvency law.

[247] Section 39.13(3)(a) of the Canada Deposit Insurance Corporation Act. Pursuant to Section 39.13(4)(a), the powers of the CDIC supersede the powers of a trustee in bankruptcy appointed under the Bankruptcy and Insolvency Act.

Luxembourg, Netherlands, Switzerland); in some of these, a regulatory receivership under the banking law is also available *(Canada, France).* In other countries, banks may be submitted only to a regulatory receivership under the banking law *(Italy, Norway, United States).*

Originally, in many countries, the banking law did not provide for a special bank receivership. Insolvent banks were submitted to general insolvency law and their licenses were revoked. Solvent banks whose licenses were revoked were liquidated in accordance with provisions of company law or continued to carry out nonregulated activities.[248] When, in some countries, the liquidation procedures under company law were found to provide insufficient safeguards for depositors and other creditors of banks or for the banking system, a special forced liquidation procedure for banks was adopted and included in the banking law to be administered by the bank regulator or by the courts.

In some countries, the application of the general insolvency law to insolvent banks had become problematic when, as a result of a national banking crisis, court systems were overwhelmed by a large number of bank insolvencies. This was used as justification for exempting banks from court-administered insolvency proceedings and submitting banks instead to an extrajudicial bank receivership.[249] The argument was reinforced by several additional considerations, including the following.

Court-administered insolvency proceedings are too time-consuming to permit the expeditious resolution of failing banks, and especially the prompt payment of depositors; both are required to maintain public confidence in the banking system and to avoid contagious runs on other banks. When a bank fails, parts of its business may have to be transferred promptly to a viable institution, in order to minimize the disruption that the failure of a banking institution can cause for the bank's depositors or in certain areas of the financial system, such as the payment, clearing, and settlement systems for foreign exchange and securities transactions; such prompt action is difficult to achieve under a court-administered general insolvency proceeding. Much of what is called the rehabilitation phase in a general insolvency proceeding con-

---

[248] See Chapter XII, Section 3, below, for a brief discussion of the effects of the revocation of the banking license.

[249] This occurred in the *United States* where the Financial Institutions Reform, Recovery, and Enforcement Act of 1989 (FIRREA) transferred the power of the courts to appoint receivers for banks to the FDIC.

sists for banks of corrective action ordered by the bank regulator; corrective action may have been more or less exhausted before a bank would enter a formal insolvency proceeding. Moreover, keeping insolvent banks open during the often lengthy rehabilitation phase of a general insolvency procedure would impair public confidence in the banking system.

A similar argument can be made with regard to judicial receiverships of banks under the banking law. For example, a sudden bank failure demands expeditious action on the part of the bank regulator in its attempt to transfer the business of the bank, including its deposits, to another bank so as to minimize the before-mentioned disruptions. The appointment of a receiver by the regulator pursuant to the banking law should take considerably less time than such appointment would take when it must be made by the courts, including the time required for preparing and presenting a petition, for issuing a notice and conducting a court hearing, and for preparing a court decision.

Prompt closure of insolvent banks helps conserve the value of bank assets for creditors, helps preserve the credibility of the bank regulator, and thereby helps diminish systemic risk. There is a link between prompt closure of insolvent banks and public confidence in the banking system. Prompt closure of insolvent banks is evidence of a decisive bank regulator and bolsters confidence in the banking system as a whole, while keeping insolvent banks open through negligent regulatory forbearance that the public perceives as weak raises doubts about the soundness of all other banks.

These arguments have been answered with counterarguments supporting a court-administered receivership for banks. Some of these are discussed below.

In most countries, judicial receivership is the rule for corporations. Therefore, moving bank receivership out of the courts and under the administration of the bank regulator is an exception that requires adequate justification.

One of the arguments used to justify regulatory bank receivership procedures is the need for prompt payment of deposits, which allegedly cannot be assured in a judicial receivership. It can be admitted that the prompt payment of depositors is an important objective in limiting depositor runs on banks, as this can undermine the banking system as a whole. However, it is in order to reduce these systemic risks that many countries protect bank deposits through deposit insurance or a special statutory preference.[250] Deposit insurance has therefore diminished the need for prompt payment of depositors by using a regulatory bank receivership.

This raises the question whether deposit insurance reduces the risk of depositor runs on banks sufficiently, i.e., to a point where this risk can no longer be used as an argument to exempt banks from judicial receivership. In several countries, there is anecdotal evidence that it does not and that the availability of deposit insurance does not prevent runs by insured depositors on banks, even though such runs may be less frequent or intense than they otherwise might be. There are several reasons for this phenomenon, depending in part on local conditions. Although deposit insurance may guarantee the eventual return of deposits, it may take a long time before insurance payments on deposits are made, and most depositors cannot wait. Meanwhile, the government may flood the economy with liquidity, driving down the real value of the unpaid deposits. Finally, there always is a risk that the state will renege on its deposit insurance obligations.

The argument that regulatory bank receivership is necessary to produce a prompt closure of banks so as to promote confidence in the banking system, although theoretically true, has little practical significance. Moving bank receivership out of the courts does little to advance payments to depositors and other creditors of banks. In practice, the liquidation of a bank can rarely be fast. Bank creditors can rarely be paid in full before a comprehensive bank audit has been completed, all claims on the bank have been verified, and the aggregate value of all assets of the bank available for payment has been determined. Because of the volume, variety, and complexity of banking transactions and the large numbers of counterparties (creditors and debtors), the liquidation of a bank, even a small one, will nearly always take considerable time, regardless of whether it is carried out under an extrajudicial bank receivership or under a court-administered receivership under the banking law or under the insolvency law.

---

[250] In the absence of a formal deposit insurance system, *Australia*: Section 13A(3) of the Banking Act 1959, gives priority to payment of a bank's deposit liabilities over all other liabilities of the bank; while *Switzerland* grants a special preference for household savings and alimony and pension deposits up to SwF 30,000—Article 37a of the Swiss Federal Law on Banks and Savings Banks. See also Article 49 of Law 21526 of *Argentina*. The *United States*: 12 U.S.C. § 1821 (d)(11)(A) protects bank deposits with a high priority, notwithstanding deposit insurance. For the purposes of this discussion, statutory preferences protecting bank deposits are deemed to be included under the term "deposit insurance."

Some serious legal disadvantages attach to regulatory receiverships for banks. These include that regulatory bank receivership denies bank creditors the procedural and substantive protection afforded by a proper judicial administration. If a regulatory bank receivership procedure is somewhat faster than a court-administered receivership, that is so because an extrajudicial procedure avoids the inevitable procedural delays of a judicial proceeding. Usually, it is characteristic of a receivership carried out under judicial administration that important decisions and actions of the receiver are subject to the prior approval of the court. This requires an *ex ante* review by the court. It is this *ex ante* character of judicial administration that affords protection to creditors.[251]

The principal disadvantage of an extrajudicial regulatory receivership is therefore that it provides no effective legal safeguards. Although the availability of an *ex post* review process may afford creditors in a regulatory receivership some protection against improper regulatory action, it generally does not present a real deterrent but only grants a right to compensation for losses suffered as a result of regulatory abuse. This disadvantage is even greater when the deposit insurance agency is appointed as receiver of an insolvent bank, because its interests as one of the bank's principal creditors raises doubts about its impartiality as receiver in administering the claims of competing creditors, undermining their confidence in the receivership process.

At this point in the argument, it should be noted that placing bank receivership under judicial administration is not without benefit for the bank regulator: a court-administered bank receivership lessens the regulator's responsibilities and potential liabilities and thereby deflects political pressure and reduces the risk of successful litigation against it.

Sometimes, a case is made for avoiding judicial administration in countries with a weak or corrupt judicial system. Indeed, it is not illogical to argue that receivership and liquidation of banks should not be administered by a judiciary that aggravates the problems of a bank insolvency, especially where it can be shown that the sloppy treatment of bank insolvencies harbors increased risks to the financial system. Nevertheless, although avoiding the judiciary might produce short-term gains in efficiency and might even reduce systemic risks, its long-term costs could be substantial. Apart from the fact that court avoidance would diminish what little respect remains for the judiciary and

---

[251] Such an *ex ante* review should be distinguished from a review *ex post* in which decisions and actions of the receiver are subject to review after they have been taken, often at the request of an interested party.

thereby weaken the rule of law, it would place banks and their creditors at the mercy of the bank regulator and its receivers, which—and this is the point—should not be expected to treat bank owners and creditors with greater equity and fairness than the judiciary. Generally, a weak judiciary is a product of a culture of disrespect for the rule of law, which is not limited to the legal community but is shared by the public at large. In extreme cases, a compromise might be found in submitting an otherwise regulatory bank receivership to the supervision of an independent judicial review panel, staffed with unbiased external accountants and other financial experts.

Meanwhile, the argument in favor of placing bank receivership under the control of the courts would not *per se* be an argument against permitting a bank receivership under the banking law instead of a receivership under general insolvency law. From the perspective of bank regulation, which is the focus of this book, a bank receivership under the banking law has important advantages over a general insolvency procedure because, more easily than a general insolvency law, the banking law can be tailored to meet the special requirements of the banking sector.

There is an even stronger argument for removing bank receivership from the general insolvency law to the banking law. General insolvency proceedings leading to the liquidation of a bank tend to place the fate of the bank into the hands of the judiciary. This raises some difficult legal policy issues. Even though the gravity of the measure may appear to require the high authority of a court, the bank regulator is the only authority technically qualified to determine if the statutory grounds for liquidating the bank concerned have been met. More important, the bank regulator, as the appointed guardian of the safety and soundness of the banking system, should be the only authority qualified to determine whether a liquidation of the bank would or would not have unacceptable adverse consequences for the banking system as a whole. A similar argument could be made for the need to involve other monetary authorities charged with the protection of the broader financial sector, including the capital markets and the payment and securities transfer systems. Allowing the judiciary to make the decision whether a bank should be liquidated, and then not necessarily on financial policy grounds but on grounds derived from general insolvency law, does not afford enough protection against overriding systemic risks.

However, there is another side to this argument. Once it is determined that an insolvent bank should not be rescued or that it cannot benefit from other bank resolution techniques, the bank must be liquidated. If in that event the bank's depositors are largely protected by deposit insurance, it is difficult to see why the bank regulator should not revoke the banking license and turn the bank over to the bankruptcy court for liquidation like any other insolvent company. Submitting insolvent banks to insolvency proceedings under the general insolvency law needs no justification. Submitting insolvent corporations to general insolvency proceedings is the rule; submitting banks to special insolvency proceedings is the exception that must be justified. If and when it is decided to turn a bank over to liquidation, that must mean that there is no overriding systemic interest in preserving the bank. With respect to a bank whose depositors benefit from deposit insurance, it is difficult to see what significant systemic interests would be adversely affected by the fact that such bank would be wound up in a court-administered general insolvency proceeding rather than in a receivership carried out under banking law.

Notwithstanding this argument, the difference between a judicial receivership under the banking law and a judicial receivership under the general insolvency law need not be so great as to offset the before-mentioned advantages of keeping bank receiverships within the framework of the banking law.

This brings us to the choice between regulatory receivership and judicial receivership under the banking law. The foregoing points to the conclusion that this choice should be driven by the search for a proper balance between concern for the soundness of the banking system and the equally legitimate need to protect the interests of bank creditors. It would appear that regulatory receivership would be justified only if systemic considerations outweigh creditor interests. This will, for instance, nearly always be the case if a bank suddenly and unexpectedly fails and a receivership serves to transfer the bank's business or at least its depository business quickly to another bank in a sale or merger, preferably over the weekend, because then efficiency and speed are at a premium.[252] The same will apply if there are urgent reasons for taking immediate control of a bank in order to stop ongoing criminal activities (money laundering) or to secure its assets for fear of their dissipation by crooked owners or managers. The argument that speed is also of the essence in a bank closure is far less convincing. Therefore, as insolvent banks move closer to liquidation and the chances of a successful restructuring or transfer of their business as a

---

[252] See Chapter XI, Section 1, below, for a brief discussion of this case.

going concern diminish, the balance of the argument begins to shift toward protection of creditor rights under a judicial receivership.

This line of reasoning suggests a regime consisting of two different receivership procedures for banks, both under the banking law: a general receivership under administration of the courts that would be the rule, and a special receivership administered by the bank regulator as the exception allowed on systemic grounds. The law should define the systemic grounds on which the special receivership procedure may be used and should authorize the bank regulator to take control of a bank, subject to ratification or termination of the receivership by the courts within a brief period of time such as one week.

IX

Provisional Administration Under the Banking Law

1. General Issues

Provisional administration, or conservatorship as it is sometimes called, is a bank administration procedure for managing and operating a bank in distress back to compliance with prudential requirements, or for preserving the value of the bank while it is being prepared for the transfer to another institution by sale or merger, or for liquidation. Although its objective is largely corrective in nature, it should be distinguished from other corrective action in that it requires taking control of a bank. It should also be distinguished from receivership whose main goals are to minimize the systemic effects of a bank failure and to preserve the value of a bank for its creditors.

Provisional administration is usually carried out under regulatory administration through one or more provisional administrators who are appointed and supervised by the bank regulator and take over part or all of the management of the bank. Provisional administration may, however, be instituted and supervised by the courts,[253] especially if it is used in conjunction with a judicial moratorium on payment of bank debt.[254]

Objectives of Provisional Administration

The principal functional objectives of provisional administration of a bank in distress are to save all or a substantial part of the bank by

---

[253] *Austria*: Articles 83–91 of the Austrian Banking Act.

[254] This is the case in *Switzerland*: Articles 29 ff. of the Federal Law on Banks and Savings Banks.

managing and operating it back to regulatory compliance, or to preserve the value of the bank while it is being prepared for transfer to
another institution, in a sale or merger, or for liquidation.

The purposes of provisional administration may be specified in the
law, either explicitly or implicitly. An example of the former is found
in the provision of *United States* law granting the FDIC, as conservator,
the power to take such action as may be

(i) necessary to put the insured depository institution in a
sound and solvent condition; and

(ii) appropriate to carry on the business of the institution and
to preserve and conserve the assets and property of the
institution.[255]

Instances of an implicit recognition of these objectives can be found in
banking law provisions that require termination of provisional administration and liquidation if the bank cannot be rescued or preserved.[256]

A bank under provisional administration continues to operate as a
going concern. This means that, to be successful, the provisional
administrator must behave like an entrepreneur, entering into new
transactions, taking and managing risks, in short, engaging in banking
activities. As a rule, where the law provides for provisional administration, provisional administrators must carry out their tasks from within
the corporate structure of the bank to which they are appointed.

There is general agreement that provisional administration should not
be misused to postpone an inevitable failure of a bank. Therefore, the
law may require as a condition for its institution a judgment that there
is a real prospect that the provisional administration would achieve its
purpose, such as the survival of the bank as a going concern.[257] In conjunction with a moratorium, the law may require that the bank to be
placed under provisional administration is not overindebted.[258]
Conversely, the law may require that a provisional administration be ter-

---

[255] 12 U.S.C. § 1821(d)(2)(D).

[256] E.g., *Portugal*: Article 152 of the Legal Framework of Credit Institutions and
Financial Companies, approved by Decree-Law No. 298/92; *Switzerland*: Article 35(2) of
the Federal Law on Banks and Savings Banks.

[257] *Austria*: Article 83(1) of the Austrian Banking Act. A similar judgment is required in
England: Section 8(3)(a) of the Insolvency Act 1986, as interpreted by the courts: *In re
Harris Simons Construction Ltd* [1989] 1 WLR 368, per Hoffmann J.; although the English
requirement applies to judicial bank rehabilitation under general insolvency law, its rationale would apply to regulatory provisional administration as well.

[258] *Switzerland*: Article 29(2) of the Federal Law on Banks and Savings Banks.

minated if either (a) the bank's deposit liabilities have been repaid or suitable provision has been made for their repayment so that provisional administration is no longer necessary; or (b) the bank is insolvent or is unlikely to be returned to solvency within a reasonable time.[259]

There is much to be said for requiring as conditions precedent to provisional administration that the goals to be pursued with such administration are defined and that a judgment is made that there is a real prospect that such goals will be achieved. For instance, if the goal of a provisional administration is to return a bank to compliance with prudential standards, realization of that goal should be judged likely before a provisional administrator is appointed for the bank. In serving transparency, this judgment should be recorded and explained in the decision and notification of appointment of the administrator. Requiring the authorities to articulate the purpose of a provisional administration and to assess the likelihood of realizing that purpose before it begins adds discipline to the process. It also helps avoid situations where an administrator would be appointed without consideration of the risk of further deterioration of the bank's condition at the expense of its creditors or, worse yet, situations where the principal objective of the appointment would be to put off an inevitable bank closure.

If the objective of the provisional administration of a bank is to manage the bank back to compliance with prudential requirements, that objective can be realized only if the regime of corrective measures to be carried out under provisional administration is fully integrated into, and carried out as an integral part of, the bank's policies and procedures. Corrective measures are intended and designed to be executed by the bank concerned as part of its operations.

Reasons Supporting Provisional Administration

The principal rationale for provisional administration is to have corrective or conservatory measures carried out by a provisional administrator, because the bank's own management is judged unwilling or unable to execute the corrective measures ordered by the bank regulator, or cannot be trusted to take the conservatory measures that are required to stabilize the bank's financial condition pending its sale, merger, or liquidation.[260]

---

[259] *Australia*: Section 13C(1) of the Banking Act 1959. Cf. *Canada*: Sections 650–652 of the Bank Act; *Portugal*: Articles 146 and 152 of the Legal Framework of Credit Institutions and Financial Companies, approved by Decree-Law No. 298/92; *Switzerland*: Article 35(2) of the Federal Law on Banks and Savings Banks.

[260] In *the Netherlands*: Article 28(3) of the Law on Supervision of the Credit System, this is the principal ground for appointing provisional administrators.

Reasons Against Provisional Administration

In several countries the law does not provide for regulatory provisional administration.[261] One practical reason may be that the bank regulator simply lacks the staff resources to manage a bank or to supervise the management of a bank by an administrator. This argument is more serious than it may seem at first glance. Bank regulators are not in the business of managing and operating banks but of exercising prudential banking supervision. Prudential banking supervision is not the same as bank management, and bank regulators do not necessarily have the qualifications, experience, or even the temperament required of a successful bank manager.

Provisional administration lends itself to abuse. Provisional administration has been used to postpone the inevitable closure of banks, for instance, owing to political pressure or because the deposit insurance system lacked the funds to pay off bank depositors. Obviously, the use of provisional administration to mask forbearance is likely to worsen the condition of the banks concerned and to increase the costs associated with their resolution to be borne by the state and by their creditors.

Finally, yet not less important, in most countries with provisional administration for banks, bank owners largely retain their rights. As a result, they could frustrate a provisional administration. Therefore, the appointment of a receiver whose powers exceed those of the provisional administrator and typically include those of the bank's owners is often preferred.

U.S. Practice

The provisional administration procedures used in the United States during the savings and loan crisis of the 1980s are illustrative of how some of the disadvantages of provisional administration can be overcome. Because the staff and other resources of the U.S. bank regulator were inadequate to resolve the relatively large number of failing savings and loan institutions, the Resolution Trust Company (RTC) was established by the U.S. Congress and charged with the merger or liquidation of savings associations previously insured by the Federal Savings and Loan Insurance Corporation that would be declared insolvent between the beginning of 1989 and mid-1995. The Federal Deposit Insurance Corporation (FDIC) became the manager of the

---

[261] *Austria, Belgium, Denmark, England, Germany, Norway,* and *Sweden.*

RTC. Of the 747 bank failures resolved by the RTC, 706 were administered under a conservatorship.[262]

As described in a report issued by the FDIC,[263] the procedures generally worked as follows:

> The conservatorship process began when the bank regulator closed an insolvent savings and loan institution and appointed the RTC as receiver. The bank regulator executed a pass-through receivership in which all deposits, substantially all assets, and certain non-deposit liabilities of the original institution instantly "passed through the receiver" to a newly chartered federal mutual association, subsequently known as "the conservatorship." The regulator then appointed the RTC as conservator of the new institution, which placed the RTC in control of the institution. To achieve its goals and objectives, the RTC assigned a managing agent and one or more asset specialists, who were also RTC employees, to the institution in conservatorship. The RTC retained the majority of the former institution's employees, who continued to perform the same functions they had before conservatorship; however, the day-to-day management and ultimate authority was given to the RTC-appointed managing agent. The managing agent's role was to ensure that management of the institution adhered to the RTC's policies and procedures, while the asset specialist would assist the managing agent with asset management and disposition.

> The objectives of the conservatorship were to (1) establish control and oversight while promoting depositor confidence; (2) evaluate the condition of the institution and determine the most cost-effective method of resolution; and (3) operate the institution in a safe and sound manner pending resolution by minimizing operating losses, limiting growth, eliminating any speculative activities, and terminating any waste, fraud, and insider abuse. Shrinking an institution by curtailing new lending activity and selling assets was also a high priority.

> At the time the conservatorship was resolved, either through a sale or deposit payoff, the institution again was placed into a receivership (the second receivership). Both receiverships, the initial pass-through receivership and the second receivership, paid unsecured creditors and other claimants on a pro rata basis according to the recoveries within each receivership.

One of the key features of this procedure is that it avoids the continued influence of bank owners by transferring most of the bank's

---

[262] FDIC, *Managing the Crisis: the FDIC and RTC Experience 1980–94*, August 1998, at p. 115.

[263] *Ibid.*, at pp. 117–18.

assets and liabilities to a new entity established for the purpose. Here, provisional administration governs not a failing bank but a failing bank's assets and liabilities.

2. Appointment of a Provisional Administrator

In several countries, the regulator is authorized to appoint a provisional administrator to a bank[264] or to take direct control of a bank.[265] In others, the provisional administrator is appointed by the courts.[266]

The grounds on which the appointment of a provisional administrator may be made vary. In some countries, the law provides for one or more general grounds of appointment of a provisional administrator. The law may authorize the appointment, for instance, when the operation of the bank on a normal basis can no longer be assured;[267] when there are serious management irregularities or violations of the law or when serious losses are predicted;[268] where the liquidity or solvency of a bank is threatened;[269] or when the bank is overindebted or insolvent.[270] The law may mandate the appointment of a provisional administrator when the bank is granted a debt-service moratorium.[271] In other countries, a provisional administrator may be appointed at the request of the management of the bank concerned.[272]

---

[264] *France*: Article 44 of Law No. 84-46 on the Activities and Supervision of Credit Institutions; *Italy*: Article 71(1) of the Law of 1993 on Matters Concerning Banking and Credit; *Netherlands*: Article 28(3) of the Law on Supervision of the Credit System; *Portugal*: Article 143(1) of the Legal Framework of Credit Institutions and Financial Companies, approved by Decree-Law No. 298/92; *United States*: 12 U.S.C. §§ 203(a) and 1821(c).

[265] *Australia*: Section 13A(1) of the Banking Act 1959; *Canada*: Section 648(1) of the Bank Act.

[266] *Austria*: Article 83(1) of the Austrian Banking Act; *Switzerland*: Articles 29(2) and 30(1) of the Federal Law on Banks and Savings Banks, in the framework of a judicial moratorium.

[267] *France*: Article 44 of Law No. 84-46 on the Activities and Supervision of Credit Institutions.

[268] *Italy*: Article 70(1) of the Law of 1993 on Matters Concerning Banking and Credit.

[269] *Australia*: Section 13A(1) of the Banking Act 1959; *Netherlands*: Article 28(1) of the Law on Supervision of the Credit System; *Spain*: Article 31 of Law 26/1988 on the Supervision and Intervention of Credit Institutions.

[270] *Austria*: Article 83(1) of the Austrian Banking Act.

[271] *Switzerland*: Articles 29(1)bis and 30(1) of the Federal Law on Banks and Savings Banks.

[272] *France*: Article 44 of Law No. 84-46 on the Activities and Supervision of Credit Institutions.

Alternatively, the law may list several distinct grounds for the appointment of a provisional administrator. For instance, the banking law of *Canada* specifies the following grounds:

a) the bank has failed to pay its liabilities or, in the opinion of the Superintendent, will not be able to pay its liabilities as they become due and payable;

b) in the opinion of the Superintendent, a practice or state of affairs exists in respect of the bank that may be materially prejudicial to the interests of the bank's depositors or creditors, or the owners of any assets under the bank's administration;

c) the assets of the bank are not, in the opinion of the Superintendent, sufficient to give adequate protection to the bank's depositors and creditors;

d) any asset appearing on the books or records of the bank or held under its administration is not, in the opinion of the Superintendent, satisfactorily accounted for;

e) the regulatory capital of the bank has, in the opinion of the Superintendent, reached a level or is eroding in a manner that may detrimentally affect its depositors or creditors;

f) the bank has failed to comply with an order of the Superintendent ....; or

g) the bank's deposit insurance has been terminated by the Canada Deposit Insurance Corporation.[273]

As the appointment of a provisional administrator is a serious and invasive measure, the law may follow a two-step procedure and require that prior notice had been given to the bank and that the bank had been ordered unsuccessfully to correct the situation within a certain time period, before a provisional administrator may be appointed;[274] the law may restrict the authority to appoint a provisional administrator to exceptionally grave conditions;[275] or the law may provide that the appointment must be made by the bankruptcy court.[276]

---

[273] *Canada*: Section 648(1.1) of the Bank Act. See for a similar list of grounds *Portugal*: Article 143(1) of the Legal Framework of Credit Institutions and Financial Companies, approved by Decree-Law No. 298/92; and, for an even longer list, *United States*: 12 U.S.C. § 1821(c)(5), including additional items such as the willful violation of a cease and desist order and money laundering.

[274] *Netherlands*: Article 28(3) of the Law on Supervision of the Credit System, although pursuant to para. (4) the regulator may in cases of urgency make the appointment without such notice and grace period.

[275] *Spain*: Article 31(1) of Law No. 26/1988 on Supervision and Intervention with respect to Credit Institutions.

[276] *Austria*: Article 83(1) of the Austrian Banking Act.

In any event, where the goal of provisional administration is to manage a bank back to compliance with prudential requirements, the administrative law principle of proportionality would appear to require that, as a rule, the provisional administrator be appointed only when less intrusive corrective action has failed or cannot reasonably be expected to restore the bank to health within a reasonable time frame. A central condition for the institution of provisional administration seems to be that the bank's management is judged unable or unwilling to take the necessary corrective or conservatory measures.

3. Legal Effects of the Appointment of a Provisional Administrator

In many countries, the appointment of a provisional administrator for a bank must be given the necessary legal effects by notifying the bank of the appointment and by announcing the appointment to the public through newspapers, the Official Gazette, or entry into the register of companies.

Powers of the Administrator

Where the provisional administrator takes control of the bank, he effectively takes over the management of the bank. This can be authorized by the law in several ways.

In most countries with provisional administration, the powers of the administrator are explicitly and formally provided for in the law. In some countries, the law attaches to the appointment of a provisional administrator the dissolution of management and grants the provisional administrator the powers and functions of the members of the board of directors of the bank (collectively and individually), including the board's powers of delegation.[277] Or the law may state that the powers of the bank's management are transferred to the provisional administrator,[278] or that the provisional administrator succeeds to all rights, titles, powers, and privileges of the bank's management and may oper-

---

[277] *Australia*: Sections 15(1) and 14A(1), respectively, of the Banking Act 1959; cf. *Italy*: Articles 70(1) and 71 of the Law of 1993 on Matters Concerning Banking and Credit where the bank's management is dissolved by decree of the Ministry of the Treasury, while the administrator is appointed by the bank regulator.

[278] *France*: Article 44 of Law No. 84-46 on the Activities and Supervision of Credit Institutions.

ate the bank with all the powers of its management.[279] Alternatively, the law may order the provisional administrator to manage and operate the bank, and may provide that the powers of the bank's managers are *ipso facto* suspended,[280] or that they may be suspended by the regulator.[281] There are cases where the law grants the provisional administrator only implicit managerial authority, for instance, when the law leaves bank management in place and provides that management may exercise its authority only after approval of the administrator and in compliance with the instructions of the administrator.[282]

In most countries where the law authorizes the appointment of a provisional administrator, it follows from the law that the provisional administrator must work within the existing corporate structure of the bank. In most of the countries reviewed, the provisional administrator has powers limited to those of bank management, and lacks the super powers that the law may grant to receivers of an insolvent bank.[283] Submitting the provisional administrator to the restrictions imposed on the powers of bank managers by company law and banking law has the legal advantage of forcing the provisional administrator to operate within the normal and therefore familiar framework of corporate governance. Bringing provisional administrators under the bank's corporate structure ensures creditors of the bank that there is a continuity of legal regime.

Yet, the very fact that existing corporate structures remain intact harbors the risk that remaining bank managers, who caused or contributed to the problems leading to provisional administration, would sabotage the work of the administrator. Therefore, removing bank management and replacing it with a provisional administrator must be preferred over alternatives that permit bank management to remain in office. Alternatively, the law may provide that if the manager of a bank under provisional administration purports to act in relation to the bank's business while a provisional administrator is in office, those acts are invalid and of no effect.[284]

---

[279] *United States*: 12 U.S.C. §§1821 (d)(2)(A)(I) and (B)(I).

[280] *Canada*: Section 649 of the Bank Act.

[281] *Portugal*: Articles 143(2) and (3) of the Legal Framework of Credit Institutions and Financial Companies, approved by Decree-Law No. 298/92.

[282] *Netherlands*: Article 28(3)(a) of the Law on Supervision of the Credit System.

[283] There are exceptions, however. See the exceptionally broad powers of the FDIC as conservator in the *United States*: 12 U.S.C. § 1821(d). In *Australia*, a provisional administrator may sell or otherwise dispose of the whole or any part of the bank's business, on any terms and conditions that the administrator considers appropriate—Section 14A(5) of the Banking Act 1959.

[284] *Australia*: Section 15(3) of the Banking Act 1959.

Competing Rights of Bank Owners

In most of the countries reviewed whose banking law provides for provisional administration, owners of a bank under provisional administration retain their rights, even though the law may authorize that restrictions be imposed on the exercise of such rights. These include the authority of the provisional administrator to veto decisions of shareholders,[285] and the authority of the bank regulator to submit decisions of the general meeting of shareholders to the prior approval of the provisional administrator.[286]

There are exceptions, however. In the *United States*, the law provides that the FDIC as provisional administrator (conservator) of a bank succeeds to all rights, titles, powers, and privileges of any stockholder or member of the bank.[287] In *Italy*, the order by which the provisional administrator is appointed has the effect of suspending the functions of the meetings of shareholders, except when the meeting is convened by the administrator.[288] In *France*, when a bank is under provisional administration, the law authorizes the court, at the request of the bank regulator made in the interest of the bank's depositors, to order some of the owners of the bank who exercise legal or factual control over the bank to dispose of their shares at a price set by the court, or to decide that for a period fixed by the court their shareholder voting rights will be exercised by a trustee appointed by the court, or to order the disposal of all shares of the bank.[289] It should be noted that the banking law may grant authority to suspend the voting rights of shareholders as a general matter, irrespective of provisional administration.[290]

Where provisional administrators must carry out their function within the corporate structure of the bank to which they are appointed and they are not vested with the powers of bank owners, shareholder consent must be obtained for all actions where this is normally

---

[285] See for a right of veto: *Austria*: Article 84(2) of the Law on the Banking System; and *Portugal*: Article 143(2)(a) of the Legal Framework of Credit Institutions and Financial Companies, approved by Decree-Law No. 298/92.

[286] *Netherlands*: Article 28(3) of the Law on Supervision of the Credit System.

[287] 12 U.S.C. § 1821(d)(2)(A).

[288] Article 70(2) of the Law of 1993 on Matters Concerning Banking and Credit.

[289] Article 46-1 of Law No. 84-46 on the Activities and Supervision of Credit Institutions. See also *Argentina*: Article 35bis(I)(c) of the Financial Institutions Law.

[290] E.g., *Austria*: Article 20(6) of the Austrian Banking Act; *Switzerland*: Article 23ter(1bis) of the Federal Law on Banks and Savings Banks; see for additional provisions the review of corrective measures affecting the rights of bank owners in Chapter V, Section 2, above.

required by company law. Consequently, in many countries, an ailing bank may not be recapitalized at the initiative of the provisional administrator without the express consent of the general meeting of shareholders.[291] This consent requirement gives bank owners a veto over corrective measures that are not in their interest. This must be regarded as the Achilles' heel of provisional administration. Innovative approaches will be needed to obtain the consent of recalcitrant bank owners while denying them free ridership. One of these is the before-mentioned authority of the courts in *France* to decide that for a certain time period shareholder voting rights are to be exercised by a trustee appointed by the court.[292] If such solutions are not available, the bank may have to be moved into receivership.

On balance, the conclusion is justified that owners should be removed as impediments to corrective measures, either by suspending their powers by court order or by vesting those powers in the provisional administrator by operation of law. Saving a bank is normally dictated by systemic considerations and the regulator, or the judiciary upon application of the regulator, should have the statutory powers to do all it takes to achieve that objective. However, it cannot be denied that, apparently, in several of the countries providing for provisional administration, society (acting through its legislature) attaches so much weight to ownership rights that it is prepared to sacrifice some efficiency and to incur some additional systemic risk in order to afford bank owners one last chance to help save their bank before their rights are formally extinguished or otherwise made illusory in a receivership.

Moratorium[293]

In some countries, the effects of provisional administration include a debt-service moratorium.[294] As a bank when it is placed under provisional administration is often still solvent, the stay imposed by the law

---

[291] See, for the countries of the *European Union*, the judgment of the European Court of Justice of March 12, 1996 in *Panagis Pafitis* v. *Trapeza Kentrikis Ellados, et al (C-441/93)*.

[292] Article 46-1 of Law No. 84-46 on the Activities and Supervision of Credit Institutions, assuming that this solution meets the standards of the judgment of the European Court in the *Panagis Pafitis* case.

[293] See Chapter VII, above, for a discussion of other more general aspects of a moratorium.

[294] *Australia*: Section 15B of the Banking Act 1959; *Austria*: Article 86(1) and (2) of the Austrian Banking Act; *Portugal*: Article 147 of the Legal Framework of Credit Institutions and Financial Companies, approved by Decree-Law No. 298/92. See also Chapter VII, above.

may be made subject to certain exceptions intended to accommodate creditors. For instance, in *Australia*, the law provides that a person cannot begin or continue a proceeding (including a cross-claim or third-party claim) in a court against a bank while a provisional administrator is in control of the bank's business, unless either the court grants leave on the ground that the person would be caused hardship if leave were not granted, or the bank regulator consents to the proceedings beginning or continuing.[295] In *Austria*, the law declares a stay with respect to prior claims from the beginning of the day following publication of the court order imposing provisional administration on a bank, and permits the court to order that, depending on the bank's financial condition, prior claims be exempt from the stay for a specified percentage or that the administrator pay off selected prior claims.[296]Conversely, in other countries, notably *Switzerland*, the appointment of a provisional administrator is not a ground for, but rather a consequence of, the institution of a debt-service moratorium for the benefit of banks.[297] The difference between provisional administration accompanied by a moratorium and a moratorium accompanied by provisional administration appears to be more one of procedure than one of substance, as the grounds for both are more or less the same and as the order depends on whether the procedure begins with the appointment of a provisional administrator or with the granting of a moratorium.

The timing of the effectiveness of a moratorium is important for payment system operators. This issue is discussed more fully below.[298]

Termination

Provisional administration would normally terminate either when its goals have been achieved and the operation of the bank can be returned to the management appointed by its owners, or when it is decided that it is unlikely that the bank will return to compliance with prudential standards or that the bank should be merged with another institution or be liquidated,[299] or that the conditions instrumental for its institution

---

[295] Section 15B of the Banking Act 1959.

[296] Articles 86(1) and (2) of the Austrian Banking Act.

[297] *Switzerland*: Articles 29(2) and 30(1) of the Federal Law on Banks and Savings Banks.

[298] See the discussion of effects of the opening of insolvency proceedings on payment systems in Chapter XIII, Section 2, below.

[299] *Australia*: Section 13C(1) of the Banking Act 1959; *Canada*: Sections 650–652 of the Bank Act; *Norway*: Sections 4-9 and 4-10 of the Law on Guarantee Schemes for Banks of 1996; *Portugal*: Article 152 of the Legal Framework of Credit Institutions and Financial Companies, approved by Decree-Law No. 298/92; *Switzerland*: Article 35(2) of the Federal Law on Banks and Savings Banks.

no longer exist.[300] The law may provide for the termination of provisional administration when bankruptcy proceedings are instituted against the bank.[301]

When, in a country where the law provides for regulatory provisional administration as well as regulatory receivership for banks (*France, Italy, United States*), the provisional administration for a bank fails, the regulator may replace it with a receivership to liquidate the bank.

The foregoing should not imply that provisional administration should last as long as it takes to achieve its goals without time limit. Therefore, it is appropriate for the law to specify deadlines for provisional administration, subject to extension.[302] Time limits impose discipline on the process, by prompting the regulator to review the prospects of provisional administration periodically and to act accordingly.

An elegant alternative is found in the banking law of *Canada*. If, 30 days after the bank regulator has taken control of the bank or its assets, the regulator receives from the bank's board of directors a notice in writing requesting the regulator to relinquish control, the regulator must, not later than 12 days after receipt of the notice, comply with the request or request the Attorney General of Canada to apply for a winding-up order in respect of the bank.[303]

---

[300] *Austria*: Article 90(2)1 of the Austrian Banking Act.

[301] *Austria*: Article 90(1) of the Austrian Banking Act.

[302] *Austria*: one year subject to extension by the regulator with the consent of the Federal Minister of Justice—Article 90(2) of the Austrian Banking Act; *Italy*: one year (or less if so specified in the decree ordering provisional administration) subject to extension up to six months in exceptional circumstances by the Minister of the Treasury at the proposal of the Bank of Italy, or an extension up to two months as required for closing the administration down—Articles 70(5) and (6) of the Law of 1993 on Banking and Credit Issues; *Netherlands*: up to two years subject to extensions of up to one year each—Article 28(5)(c) of the Law on Supervision of the Credit System; *Norway*: one year although the Ministry of Finance may stipulate a different period—Section 4-10(1) of the Law on Guarantee Schemes for Banks of 1996.

[303] Section 652 of the Bank Act. The winding-up order is applied for under the Winding-up and Restructuring Act, a special insolvency law that is applicable to banks in lieu of general insolvency law.

X

Receivership Under the Banking Law

1. General Issues

As treated in this book, receivership is a bank administration procedure for the restructuring or the closure and liquidation of banks by a receiver. It should be distinguished from rehabilitation and bankruptcy procedures under general insolvency law, even though the receivership provisions found in the banking law are often derived from provisions of the general insolvency law or include provisions of the general insolvency law by reference. It should also be distinguished from provisional administration.

Receivership can be carried out either under regulatory administration where the receiver is appointed and supervised by the bank regulator, or under judicial administration where the receiver is appointed and supervised by the courts. The principal bank resolution procedures used in a receivership are treated below in this chapter.

Objectives of Receivership

The functional objective of a receivership for a bank is to maximize the value of the bank for its creditors, including the government (if it has provided exceptional financial support to the bank) and the deposit insurance agency. The objective may be achieved by saving the business of the bank as a going concern pending its transfer to another institution in a sale or merger, or by closing and liquidating the bank, under the authority of a receiver appointed by the bank regulator or the court. Usually, upon completion of this process, the bank's operating license is revoked. For practical purposes, the effects of a regulatory bank receivership may be compared with those of a formal insolvency proceeding.

Advantages of Receivership over Provisional Administration

In most countries where the banking law provides for a receivership, these advantages are mainly that, whereas under provisional administration bank owners largely retain their rights, under receivership the rights of the bank's owners are suspended or vested in the receiver and the receiver can exercise superpowers of a trustee in bankruptcy. Accordingly, the receiver is usually granted full control over the business of the bank and relative freedom in restructuring the bank and negotiating transfers of the bank's business at terms that are most favorable for the bank's creditors, including the deposit insurance agency, without requiring shareholders consent.[304]

For these reasons and from a systemic viewpoint, a bank receivership is much to be preferred over provisional administration. Even if, after a receiver is appointed, it were decided to save the bank as a going concern in the same manner as under provisional administration, the receiver would generally have the authority to do so.

Applicable Statute

Typically, a bank receivership is carried out pursuant to provisions of banking law (*France, Italy, Luxembourg, Netherlands, Norway, Switzerland, United States*),[305] provisions of a general or special insolvency law (*Austria, Belgium, Canada, Denmark, England, France, Germany, Netherlands, Switzerland*), or provisions of company law (*Australia*).[306] In several countries (*France, Switzerland*), the law offers two receiverships for banks: solvent banks are liquidated by a receiver appointed under the banking law or the company law, for instance, when their banking license has been revoked for reasons unrelated to their financial condition, while insolvent banks are liquidated by a receiver appointed by the courts under insolvency law;[307] in the

---

[304] In countries where provisional administration is regulatory in nature while receivership is a form of judicial administration (*Luxembourg, Netherlands*), there will be a trade-off between regulatory control accompanied by limited powers and judicial control accompanied by extensive powers.

[305] Here, banking law is understood to include deposit insurance legislation.

[306] See for references to company law: *Australia*: Section 14F of the Banking Act 1959 referring to the Corporations Law of a State or internal Territory under which the bank is incorporated, which includes provisions of general insolvency law.

[307] *France*: Articles 46 and 46-2 of Law No. 84-46 on the Activities and Supervision of Credit Institutions, and Grenouilloux and Fernandez-Bollo, "France," at p. 58; *Switzerland*: Articles 23quinquies and 36 of the Federal Law on Banks and Savings Banks; and Merz and Raggenbass, "Switzerland," at p. 220.

Netherlands, the law provides for forced bank liquidation by a receiver of insolvent banks under both the general insolvency law and the banking law.[308] In a third group of countries (*Italy, Luxembourg, Norway, United States*), forced liquidation in a receivership for both solvent and insolvent banks is carried out under banking law only.[309]

Where bank receiverships are governed by the banking law, a more or less comprehensive set of rules and procedures governing forced liquidation is usually included in the banking law, either in the form of special liquidation provisions for banks,[310] or by incorporating provisions of general insolvency law into the banking law by reference,[311] or both.[312]

2. Appointment of a Receiver

In some countries where the banking law provides for a bank receivership, the receiver is appointed by the court, often at the request of the bank regulator.[313]

In other countries, receivers for a bank are not appointed by the court but by the bank regulator,[314] or by another governmental authority. In *Italy*, the receiver is appointed by the bank regulator following a decree of the Minister of the Treasury revoking the banking license and ordering the forced liquidation of the bank.[315] Similarly, in *Norway*, the receiver is an administration board appointed by the regulator follow-

---

[308] *Netherlands*: Articles 71 ff. of the Law on Supervision of the Credit System.

[309] E.g., *Italy*: Article 80 of the Law of 1993 on Matters Concerning Banking and Credit; *Luxembourg*: Article 61 of the Law on the Financial Sector; *Norway*: Section 4–10(1) of the Law of 1996 on Guarantee Schemes for Banks. In *Italy* and *Luxembourg*, liquidation of banks under insolvency law is explicitly excluded, *ibid*.

[310] See, e.g., the extensive liquidation provisions in the banking laws of *Italy*: Articles 80 ff. of the Law of 1993 on Matters Concerning Banking and Credit; *Luxembourg*: Article 60 of the Law on the Financial Sector; *United States*: 12 U.S.C. § 1821(d).

[311] E.g., *Norway*: Section 4-10(2) of the Law of 1996 on Guarantee Schemes for Banks.

[312] E.g., *Netherlands*: Articles 73–80 of the Law on Supervision of the Credit System.

[313] *Luxembourg*: Article 61 of the Law on the Financial Sector; *Netherlands*: Article 71 of the Law on Supervision of the Credit System.

[314] *France*: Article 46 of Law No. 84-46 on Activities and Supervision of Credit Institutions; *United States*: 12 U.S.C. § 191.

[315] Articles 80(1) and 81(1) of the Law of 1993 on Matters Concerning Banking and Credit; both the ministerial decree and the regulator's decision must be published in the Official Gazette.

ing a royal decree placing the bank under receivership.[316] In *Canada*, the Canada Deposit Insurance Corporation (CDIC) is appointed as receiver of federal banks by order of the Governor in Council, upon the recommendation of the Minister of Finance (supervising the bank regulator).[317] In the *United States*, the Federal Deposit Insurance Corporation (FDIC) may appoint itself as receiver of an insured depository institution after consultation with its bank regulator; the FDIC may accept the appointment by state authorities as receiver of insured state-chartered depository institutions.[318]

The statutory grounds for the appointment of a receiver often center on the actual or imminent insolvency of a bank. In banking law, three types of criteria are used to determine a bank's insolvency. Under standards of the first type, built on general bankruptcy law criteria, a bank may be deemed insolvent when it is established that the bank is unable to pay its obligations as they are due and payable and has no current prospect of being able to do so; this condition is also known as liquidity insolvency.[319] The second type of standard is known as balance sheet insolvency; it is used to declare a bank insolvent when the bank's balance sheet shows a deficit.[320] The third type of standard is regulatory insolvency; according to this standard, a bank may be deemed insolvent when its capital is no longer adequate to comply with prudential capital adequacy standards.[321] Both the second and third types of standard use the value of assets on the bank's balance sheet; as this means that these assets must be recorded at appropriate values, rules applicable to bank balance sheets in general or the valuation of bank balance sheet assets in particular may be set by law or regulation.

As receivership is the ultimate intrusion into a bank's business and in keeping with the administrative law principle of proportionality, the law may make the appointment of a receiver subject to a determina-

---

[316] Section 4-7 of the Law on Guarantee Schemes for Banks of 1996.

[317] Section 39.13(1)(b) of the Canada Deposit Insurance Corporation Act.

[318] *United States*: 12 U.S.C. § 1821(c)(10) and 12 U.S.C. § 1821(c)(3), respectively.

[319] *England*: Section 59(1)(a) of the Banking Act 1987; *Norway*: Section 4-5(1) of the Law on Guarantee Schemes for Banks of 1996.

[320] *Netherlands*: Article 77 of the Law on Supervision of the Credit System, as bankruptcy ground for banks.

[321] *Norway*: Section 4-5(1) of the Law on Guarantee Schemes for Banks of 1996; *United States*: 12 U.S.C. § 1831o(h)(3)(A) for the appointment of a receiver to a bank that is "critically undercapitalized," which by Section 1831o(b)(1) is defined as failing to meet any of the capital adequacy levels specified by Section 1831o(c)(3)(A).

tion by the bank regulator that the bank cannot be restored to compliance through regulatory corrective action.[322]

Generally, the law uses permissive language in phrasing the grounds for the appointment of a receiver. There are countries, however, where in certain circumstances the law makes the appointment of a receiver for a bank mandatory, for instance, when the bank's banking license has been revoked.[323]

Once the decision has been made that a receiver should be appointed, the appointment should be made without delay.[324] The receiver should immediately take control of the bank's assets and its books, make an assessment of the bank's financial condition for the regulator, and recommend to the regulator or the court a course of action. Preferably, a receivership is carried out in accordance with a plan of action.[325]

If a receivership is not preceded by provisional administration, the tasks of the receiver need not be limited to the liquidation of the bank but may be extended to include an attempt to save the bank as a going concern[326] or to sell the bank to, or merge it with, another institution. The following provisions of the law of *Norway* may serve as an illustration of such extended tasks of a receiver:

(1) The administration board (receiver) shall endeavour as rapidly as possible to draw up arrangements enabling the continued operation of the institution's activities on a sufficient financial basis, or seek to bring about a merger with, or have its activities transferred to, other institutions, or wind up the institution.

(2) The administration board shall as soon as possible prepare internal guidelines for the institution's operation. The board shall ensure that a liquidation committee is established which the board can consult, and the board may engage experts to assist in liquidation.

(3) Decisions of material significance to the institution require Kredittilsynet's (the regulator's) approval before they are implemented.

---

[322] *Canada*: Section 39.1(1)(b) of the Canada Deposit Insurance Corporation Act.

[323] *Luxembourg*: Article 61(1)(c) of the Law on the Financial Sector.

[324] Delay in appointing a receiver to take control of a failing bank and to preserve its assets may cause a decline in value of the bank's assets and franchise; in some jurisdictions, the resulting losses may expose the regulator to damage suits by bank creditors.

[325] See Chapter VIII, Section 3, above.

[326] If the bank is insolvent, saving its business as a going concern would generally be justified only in exceptional circumstances, for instance, where the bank is deemed too big to fail.

(4) The administration board shall within three months of its appointment provide Kredittilsynet with an assessment of the institution's position and present a plan for the further work of the board. Kredittilsynet may extend this period.

(5) The auditor shall examine the conduct by the financial institution of its business and prepare an audit report.[327]

3. Legal Effects of the Appointment of a Receiver

In many countries, the appointment of a receiver for a bank must be given the necessary external legal effects by notifying the bank of the appointment and by announcing the appointment to the public through newspapers or the Official Gazette or entry into the register of companies.

Powers of the Receiver

As a rule, the powers of a receiver include not only the powers of the bank's management but also the powers of its owners. Thus, for example, the law may provide that the powers of the organs of the bank are exclusively exercised by the receiver,[328] or that the bank's organs are suspended or become inoperative and the receiver assumes the authority vested in them.[329] In some countries the powers of the receiver also include some of the superpowers of a trustee in bankruptcy;[330] thus, the law may grant special powers to transfer liabilities and provide for the binding effect of the assumption of debt obligations on the creditors concerned without their agreement.[331]

Ownership Rights

In countries with bank receivership, a common feature of the receivership is that it effectively terminates the rights of the bank's

---

[327] Section 4-8 of the Law on Guarantee Schemes for Banks of 1996.

[328] *Netherlands*: Article 72(1) of the Law on Supervision of the Credit System.

[329] *Canada*: Section 39.14(1) of the Canada Deposit Guarantee Corporation Act; *Norway*: Article 4-6(1)(a) of the Law of 1996 on Guarantee Schemes for Banks.

[330] *Canada*: Sections 39.13(2) and (3) and 39.2 of the Canada Deposit Insurance Corporation Act; *Italy*: Article 90 of the Law of 1993 on Matters Concerning Banking and Credit; *Netherlands*: Article 75 of the Law on Supervision of the Credit System; *United States*: 12 U.S.C. § 1821(e).

[331] *Italy*: Article 90(2) of the Law of 1993 on Matters Concerning Banking and Credit; *Netherlands*: Article 75(1) of the Law on Supervision of the Credit System.

owners to their bank, if not legally, then in an economic sense. This is done not only to deny existing bank owners a free ride at the expense of the state budget, but also and especially to facilitate transfers of the bank's business and other financial measures that are required to maximize the value of the bank for its creditors, without the need to obtain shareholder consent.

The law may achieve this result by suspending the rights of the bank's shareholders,[332] or by providing that the receiver shall exclusively exercise all powers of the bank's organs (including the general meeting of shareholders).[333] In the *United States*, the FDIC, as receiver and by operation of law, succeeds to all rights, titles, powers, and privileges of any stockholder or member of the bank under receivership.[334] And if the law does not provide for such succession, it may be provided by government decision, as in *Canada* where the Governor in Council may by order vest the shares and subordinated debt of the bank in the CDIC as receiver.[335] In *France*, when a bank is under receivership, the law authorizes the court, at the bank regulator's request made in the interest of the bank's depositors, to order some owners of the bank who exercise legal or factual control over the bank to dispose of their shares at a price set by the court, or to decide that for a period fixed by the court their shareholder voting rights will be exercised by a trustee appointed by the court, or to order the disposal of all shares of the bank.[336]

Moratorium[337]

In accordance with principles of general insolvency law, the banking law may attach to bank receivership an automatic stay of debt-service payments by, or legal proceedings against, the bank concerned.[338] In

---

[332] *Italy*: Article 80(5) of the Law of 1993 on Matters Concerning Banking and Credit; *Norway*: Section 4-6(1)(a) of the Law of 1996 on Guarantee Schemes for Banks.

[333] *Netherlands*: Article 72(1) of the Law on Supervision of the Credit System.

[334] 12 U.S.C. § 1821(d)(2)(A).

[335] Section 39.13(1)(a) of the Canada Deposit Insurance Corporation Act.

[336] *France*: Article 46-1 of Law No. 84-46 on the Activities and Supervision of Credit Institutions. See also *Argentina*: Article 35bis(i)(c) of the Financial Institutions Law.

[337] See Chapter VII, above, for a discussion of other more general aspects of a moratorium.

[338] *Canada*: but under banking law only where the shares of a bank are vested in the CDIC or the CDIC is appointed as a receiver for a bank, Section 39.15(1) of the Canada Deposit Insurance Corporation Act; *Italy*: Article 83(1) of the Law of 1993 on Matters of Banking and Credit; *Luxembourg*: Article 61(4) of the Law of 1993 on the Financial Sector; *Netherlands*: Article 74(1) of the Law on Supervision of the Credit System; *United States*: 12 U.S.C. § 1821(d)(13)(C) and (D).

some countries, a stay of judicial actions and proceedings may be obtained from the courts.[339] Claims resulting from activities conducted during the moratorium and certain financial contracts or claims secured by collateral may be excluded from the moratorium.[340]

The timing of the effectiveness of a moratorium is important for payment system operators. This issue is discussed more fully below.[341]

Appeal Against Decisions of Receiver

Where the receivership is carried out under judicial supervision, appeals against decisions of the receiver would normally be brought in the court administering the receivership.

In case of regulatory receivership without judicial supervision, the law may offer special judicial procedures for remedial action by interested parties, especially where it concerns the disallowance of their claims.[342]

Termination

A receivership should terminate when its objectives have been accomplished or when the bank under receivership is submitted to judicial proceedings under the general insolvency law. In *France*, the powers of a liquidator appointed by the regulator under the banking law terminate when the bank in liquidation becomes insolvent and the liquidator must cede control of the bank to a receiver appointed by the court under the general insolvency law.[343]

One of the arguments most frequently used in support of an extra-judicial receivership is that it ensures a speedier bank resolution than proceedings under general insolvency law. If this argument is valid, the law should set a time limit to an extrajudicial receivership, after which the bank must be turned over to the bankruptcy court. This is provided

---

[339] *United States*: 12 U.S.C. § 1821(d)(12); the court must grant the stay when properly requested.

[340] *Canada*: Section 39.15(6) and (7) of the Canada Deposit Insurance Corporation Act; *Netherlands*: Article 74(2) of the Law on Supervision of the Credit System.

[341] See the discussion of effects of the opening of insolvency proceedings on payment systems in Chapter XIII, Section 2, below.

[342] *Italy*: Article 87 of the Law of 1993 on Matters Concerning Banking and Credit; *United States*: 12 U.S.C. § 1821(d)(6) and (7).

[343] Grenouilloux and Fernandez-Bollo, "France," at p. 58; see for the case where an insolvent bank loses its banking license: Article 46-2 of Law No. 84-46 on the Activities and Supervision of Credit Institutions.

for in *Canada*, where the Canada Deposit Insurance Corporation has 60 days to complete its activities concerning a bank whose shares have been vested in the CDIC, before proceedings must be initiated for the bank's liquidation under the Winding-up and Restructuring Act.[344]

---

[344] Section 39.22 of the Canada Deposit Insurance Corporation Act, which also provides that the Governor in Council may extend the 60-day period up to a total period of 180 days.

XI

Bank Resolution Procedures Used in a Banking Law Receivership

1. Principle Procedures

Bank resolution procedures are used to dispose of a bank. Generally, therefore, they come into play only while the bank is in receivership or when insolvency proceedings have been opened against the bank.[345] For the sake of the following discussion, it will be assumed that the bank is in receivership.

From a legal perspective, bank resolution procedures include special financial support; merger; purchase and assumption transactions, including the use of bridge banks; and closure, including forced liquidation and license revocation.

- Special financial support includes all forms of official open bank assistance discussed in Chapter VI, above.

- Merger of a bank means the sale of the bank's share capital to another institution.

- Purchase and assumption transactions involve the transfer of a whole bank including substantially all of its assets and liabilities, or part of a bank's assets and liabilities, to another institution. These are discussed in this chapter of the book.

---

[345] There are exceptions. Bank resolutions may also be used to dispose of part of the business of a bank in distress so that a smaller bank that remains can be successfully rehabilitated. In such cases, bank resolution procedures may be used under provisional administration, although the limited powers of a provisional administrator may require that the procedures are approved by bank owners.

- Closure of a bank involves the bank's forced liquidation and the revocation of its banking license. Forced liquidation is discussed in this chapter of the book, while license revocation is treated in the next chapter.

Dealing with a failing bank requires exceptional speed. After a receiver has taken control of the bank's assets and its books, and it is decided that the bank cannot be rehabilitated, the first order of business is to try to realize the highest market value for the bank by selling it as a going concern. Generally speaking, if a bank's business cannot be transferred to another financial institution within a week or so after commencement of the receivership, the bank's chances of being kept open on a going-concern basis will be slim and in all likelihood the bank will have to be closed. During the liquidation phase, it would still be possible to sell part of the bank's business under a purchase and assumption transaction.

Ideally, a failing bank is closed on Friday afternoon after close of business, is acquired by another bank over the weekend, and opens its doors early Monday morning under another name. If such a transaction cannot be done for the whole bank, the authorities should at least attempt to engineer a quick transfer of the bank's insured deposit liabilities to a creditworthy institution so as to minimize the effects of the bank's failure on its depositors and the attendant systemic risks. An instructive example of this process is the acquisition of Barings by the Dutch ING Group in England, even though the process took a few more days to complete.

Unlike most companies, banks do not respond well to a drawn-out resolution process under the protective umbrella of a moratorium of some sort. Once a bank has been found in need of protection from its creditors, trust in the bank and its ability to attract deposits or capital market funding will often be lost.

The law may require that, in considering the various strategies for bank resolution, the authorities conduct a careful cost-benefit analysis to determine the least-cost solution for winding up a failing bank.[346]

Although the least-cost test is theoretically attractive, it is difficult to administer in practice, *inter alia,* for the following reasons. The test requires comparisons between the costs of various resolution scenarios, such as recapitalizing the bank, merging the bank with another institution, or closing the bank. The costs of these different strategies must

---

[346] *United States*: 12 U.S.C. § 1823(c)(4).

largely be determined on the basis of estimates based on assumptions supported by hypotheses, not even counting the costs associated with the failure of strategies that aim at saving the bank.

Actually, saving a bank may often be excluded by the least-cost test. If so, special financial support to banks that are deemed too big to fail would be excluded. Logically, the costs to be considered should include not only the financial cost of possible resolution strategies to the bank regulator and the deposit insurance agency but also and especially the economic costs of a bank failure. An option that does not present the least cost to the deposit insurance agency may nevertheless be justified and even indicated by systemic considerations. So as to avoid too rigid an application of the least-cost rule, the banking law may allow exceptions; and, so as to avoid the exception's becoming the rule, the law may require super majorities for the consent of senior government officials before other than least-cost solutions are adopted.[347]

As bank owners are entitled to the distribution among them of any positive value that would remain if the bank had been broken up in a traditional liquidation of its assets, they have a residual interest in the resolution strategy to be followed. Therefore, the reasonably estimated liquidation value of the bank could be used as a supplemental benchmark for assessing the appropriateness of other resolution strategies.

2. Bank Merger

In some countries, the rights of shareholders to an insolvent bank are vested in the receiver.[348] In others, shareholders of an insolvent bank can be forced by court order to transfer their shares.[349] Both permit the authorities to arrange for the merger or sale of the banking corporation in its entirety. Mergers can be voluntary or can be assisted by the government.

The chief advantages of a bank merger include that it builds on the fact that the acquisition of an existing banking franchise is attractive

---

[347] See, e.g., the *United States*: 12 U.S.C. § 1823 (c)(4)(G) requiring a decision of the Secretary of the Treasury (in consultation with the U.S. President) pursuant to a written recommendation adopted by a two-thirds majority of both the Board of Directors of the FDIC and the Board of Governors of the Federal Reserve System.

[348] E.g., *United States*: 12 U.S.C. § 1821(d)(2)A.

[349] E.g., *France*: Article 46-1 of Law No. 84-46 on the Activities and Supervision of Credit Institutions.

to other banks that wish to expand their operations; that the activities of the failing bank can largely continue, albeit under the corporate roof of another institution, avoiding disruptions in banking services and in payment, clearing, and settlement systems; that the sales price obtained for the bank can include the bank's franchise value or goodwill, which could not be recovered if the bank were closed; and that the packaged transfer of assets and liabilities is more efficient than a traditional bank liquidation in which assets and liabilities are processed separately and individually. The chief risk of a bank merger is that an otherwise sound bank would be significantly weakened by the purchase of an undercapitalized or insolvent bank.

Alternatively, the authorities may have the power to sell all or part of the business of the bank including its assets and liabilities in a so-called purchase and assumption transaction (see Section 3 below).[350] After all assets and liabilities have been removed from a bank, the empty corporate shell remaining may yet have value to a corporate buyer, for instance, when previous losses of the acquired bank may be used as corporate income tax deductions.

3. Purchase and Assumption Transactions

Purchase and assumption transactions represent what possibly is the most common technique for realizing a going-concern value for a bank's creditors. In such transactions, another bank purchases assets and assumes liabilities of the failing bank, including preferably its goodwill and customer base. The law may contain specific authority for the receiver of a bank to engage in such transactions, sometimes subject to substantive or procedural conditions.[351]

Ideally, purchase and assumption transactions serve to transfer the entire business of the bank. Such *whole-bank* transactions include all the assets and liabilities of the failing bank; this has the advantage of moving the burden of collection on nonperforming loans to the purchasing bank. Such whole-bank transactions are similar to bank mergers and have basically the same advantages and risks. The difference

---

[350] E.g., *Netherlands*: Article 75 of the Law on Supervision of the Credit System.

[351] *Canada*: Section 39.2 of the Canada Deposit Insurance Corporation Act; *Italy*: Article 90(2) of the Law of 1993 Matters Concerning Banking and Credit; *Netherlands*: Article 75(1) of the Law on Supervision of the Credit System; *United States*: 12 U.S.C. § 1821(d)(2)(G).

between the two types of transaction is chiefly that, whereas a merger is done through a sale of equity shares, a purchase and assumption transaction consists of a sale of bank assets and a transfer and assumption of bank liabilities, each of which may require different legal steps.

As part of a purchase and assumption transaction, certain incentives may have to be offered to the buyer, such as temporary exemptions from some prudential requirements, while the deposit insurance agency may have to cover deficits between the assets and liabilities of the failing bank, less its franchise value, by a cash transfer to the acquiring bank.

Often, however, no institution can be found to acquire all of a failing bank's assets and liabilities, because the transaction is done too soon to permit a complete appraisal of those assets and liabilities and banks are understandably loath to acquire open-ended liabilities. To meet such concerns, two techniques have been developed. One is the so-called *clean-bank* purchase and assumption transaction in which only "clean" assets and "known" liabilities are transferred; "dirty" assets and open-ended liabilities that remain may be transferred to an asset management corporation, also called *bad bank*, to be processed separately. The other technique has the deposit insurance corporation write a *put option* to the acquiring bank that entitles the latter to return to the former, within a specified time period, certain assets at an agreed price.

Purchase and assumption transactions include the transfer and assumption of a bank's liabilities. Generally, the law of obligations provides that the assumption of liabilities by a third party will not bind the creditor without his consent. Obtaining the consent of all of a bank's creditors under a wholesale purchase and assumption transaction would cause substantial delays before the transaction could be closed. Therefore, the law may provide for a procedure whereby a receiver can transfer a bank's liabilities without creditor consent after obtaining prior approval from the court or the bank regulator and after publication of the transfer of liabilities. Thus, for example, in the *Netherlands*, the law provides that an assumption of bank debt in a bank receivership binds bank creditors if the court authorizes the assumption of debt and the receiver publishes the assumption of debt in the Official Gazette.[352] In other countries, the law prescribes a sim-

---

[352] *Netherlands*: Articles 75(1), (4), and (5) of the Law on Supervision of the Credit System.

ilar procedure, except that the assumption of debt may be authorized by the bank regulator.[353] Or the law simply provides that liability transfers may be made by the receiver without any approval or consent with respect to such transfer.[354]

In the *United States*, the banking regulators have the option of using bridge bank powers as part of the receivership process.[355] When one or more banks are insolvent or in danger of becoming insolvent, the Federal Deposit Insurance Corporation (FDIC) may, at its discretion, organize a new national bank that the Comptroller of the Currency is then required to charter (bridge bank). To date, this authority has been used to facilitate sales of large banks that were first closed, for which the FDIC was appointed as receiver. The sales consist of purchase and assumption transactions entered into between the FDIC as receiver and the newly chartered bridge bank. Thereafter, the bridge bank continues to operate the business of the failed bank, while the owners of the failed bank are left with an empty corporate shell.

As far as depositors and other customers of the bank are concerned, there is a seamless transition between the failed bank and the bridge bank, since, as a result of the purchase and assumption transaction, in a practical and economic sense, the doors of the bank never close. The bridge bank is controlled by the FDIC, which appoints its board of directors and may provide operating funds in lieu of capital (no capital is required for a bridge bank by law) or financial assistance, such as grants, loans, or guarantees. The law does not clearly regulate the ownership of a bridge bank. The law provides that no capital stock need be issued on behalf of a bridge bank and that a bridge bank is not an agency, establishment, or instrumentality of the United States; however, as bridge banks are organized by the FDIC and as all their ownership rights, including the issue of capital stock and their sale or merger, are exercised by the FDIC, it may be assumed that the FDIC is the owner of the bridge bank. The duration of the bridge bank is limited to a two-year period followed by no more than three one-year extensions.

The use of bridge bank powers allows the FDIC to stabilize a large bank suffering from a depositor run, clean its balance sheet through

---

[353] *Canada*: Section 39.2(1), (3), (5), and (6) of the Canada Deposit Insurance Corporation Act; *Italy*: Articles 90(2) and 58(2) and (4) of the Law of 1993 on Matters Concerning Banking and Credit.

[354] *United States*: Section 12 U.S.C. § 1821(d)(2)(G).

[355] 12 U.S.C. §§ 1821(d)(2)(F)(ii) and 1821(n).

the use of a receivership, and then enter into a bidding process by which interested parties can do due diligence prior to making an offer to purchase the bridge bank, either in a whole-bank or clean-bank purchase and assumption transaction, and without interference of owners of the failed bank. The bridge is then closed a second time; if the bridge bank was sold in a clean-bank transaction, the FDIC would administer a second receivership for the unsold assets and liabilities.

4. Forced Bank Liquidation

Generally, the law provides for three categories of bank liquidation: voluntary liquidation, forced liquidation, and liquidation in bankruptcy. Only the second one will be discussed in this section.[356]

Forced bank liquidation is a procedure for winding up all or part of a bank that cannot be rehabilitated or benefit from one or more of the preceding bank resolution procedures. Forced bank liquidation is generally carried out through the liquidation of assets and the discharge of liabilities. Although forced liquidation is usually applied to insolvent banks, it may also be used to liquidate solvent banks whose banking license is revoked because they failed to comply with nonfinancial requirements of the law, such as prohibitions of money laundering.

If provisional administration or receivership for a bank fails to manage the bank back into compliance with prudential standards, or fails to arrange for a transfer of the bank as a going concern, the bank should generally be liquidated.

Bank liquidation under general or special insolvency law is generally carried out by receivers appointed and supervised by the court. Conversely, bank liquidation under company law will generally not be subject to judicial administration; however, in case bank liquidators appointed under the company law cannot ensure an orderly liquidation, the law may provide for their replacement by court-appointed liquidators upon request of the bank regulator.[357] As was noted in the discussion of bank receivership, forced bank liquidation under the

---

[356] Voluntary bank liquidation is carried out by or at the request of the bank concerned, with the consent and usually under the supervision of the bank regulator. Consent will be denied if the bank is deemed insolvent. As it is mostly unrelated to the topic of this report, voluntary liquidation will not be further discussed.

[357] *Austria*: Article 6(5) of the Austrian Banking Act.

banking law will be carried out under a receivership that may or may not be administered by the courts.

If the liquidation is carried out in a regulatory receivership without court supervision, there is less assurance that the legitimate interests of creditors and owners of the bank are taken into account than in a judicial receivership. This is especially the case when the liquidation is administered by the deposit insurance agency (*Norway, United States*), which may have a conflict of interests between its trustee role as receiver and its position as a major creditor of the bank following subrogation to the rights of depositors after payments out of the deposit insurance fund.

XII

Revocation of the Banking License

1. Grounds to Revoke the Banking License

For a bank, the revocation of its banking license signals the end of its life as a bank. Except for banks whose corporate charter and banking license are combined in one instrument,[358] the revocation of the banking license would normally not signal the end of the bank as a corporation; rather, revocation of a bank's license means revocation of its authority to engage in core banking activities—taking deposits from the public and using them to make loans. As a bank's activities usually include other activities not requiring a banking license, there is at least a question whether the former bank should not be permitted to continue these other activities as a corporation without a banking license.[359]

In some countries, the law covers the main regulatory measures—corrective action, taking control of a bank, and license revocation—under the same grounds.[360] The same is true where and to the extent that the law formulates regulatory measures as limits or conditions attaching to the banking license.[361] In other countries, the law gives special grounds for revocation of the banking license. Accordingly, the

---

[358] E.g., in *Canada*, banks may be incorporated by letters patent issued by the Minister of Finance and come into existence on the date provided therefor in its letters patent—Sections 22 and 32 of the Bank Act. Although an existing corporation may be continued as a bank through the issuance of letters patent to it, Section 36 of the Bank Act provides that such corporation becomes a bank as if it had been incorporated under the Bank Act and that the letters patent are deemed to be the incorporating instrument of the continued bank.

[359] This question is briefly addressed *infra,* Section 3.

[360] *Belgium*: Article 57(1)(4) of the Law on the Statute and Supervision of Credit Institutions.

[361] *England*: Sections 11 and 12 of the Banking Act 1987.

banking license may be revoked—for instance, when the bank violates a provision of the banking law or regulations, or disregards a guideline, warning, or agreement made pursuant to the banking law;[362] or only when such violations are exceptionally serious;[363] or when the interests of the bank's depositors or other creditors are threatened;[364] or when the bank is no longer meeting its obligations as they mature.[365] Several banking laws authorize revocation of the banking license on the ground that continuation of the authority to conduct banking activities would not be in the public interest.[366] Generally, the grounds for license revocation are broadly phrased because it is impossible for the legislature to foresee all possible circumstances in which a bank should be closed.

Sometimes, the law sets standards in the form of statutory presumptions that a certain ground for regulatory action exists if one of the standards is met. Thus, for instance, in *Germany*, revocation of the banking license is authorized when there is a danger that the bank will be unable to meet its obligations toward its creditors; the law then provides that such danger exists, *inter alia*, if the bank loses half of its capital, reserves, and surplus, or if the bank has lost 10 percent of its capital, reserves, and surplus during each of the last three years.[367]

Insolvency *per se* does not always provide sufficient justification for revocation of the banking license. Neither does a court order opening insolvency proceedings under insolvency law. The reason is that the bank might yet be rescued or be transferred to another institution. In several countries, the law requires for the revocation of a bank's license a finding by the bank regulator that corrective measures specified in the banking law could not ensure the viability of the bank.[368] This seems a proper approach as it requires the regulator to conduct a final review of the chances of success of corrective action. However, if the

---

[362] *France*: Article 45 of Law No. 84-46 on the Activities and Supervision of Credit Institutions.

[363] *Italy*: Article 80(1) of the Law of 1993 on Matters Concerning Banks and Credit.

[364] *England*: Section 11(1)(e) of the Banking Act 1987, but only for interests of depositors and potential depositors; *Germany*: Section 35(2)(4) of the Law on the Credit System; *Netherlands*: Article 15(1)(d) *juncto* Article 9(1)(c), of the Law on Supervision of the Credit System.

[365] *Austria*: Section 6(2) of the Austrian Banking Act.

[366] *Australia*: Section 9A(2)(b) of the Banking Act 1959; *Norway*: Section 8 of the Act on Commercial Banks of 1961.

[367] Article 35(2)(4) of the Law on the Credit System.

[368] *Austria*: Section 70(4)3 of the Austrian Banking Act; *Germany*: Article 35(2)(4) of the Law on the Credit System.

finding would be required for all banks in distress, it would implicitly impose on the regulator the duty to do for every bank all that is within its power to save it, which obviously would go too far.

Generally, the law provides a reasonable degree of discretion to the bank regulator for revoking a banking license by including broadly phrased grounds for license revocation and thereby leaving room for judgment. In this area of bank regulation, regulatory discretion is important, for several reasons. The revocation of a banking license requires careful judgment, based on the particular circumstances of each case, because the decision to revoke the license of a bank is final, and practically irrevocable as the law normally requires prompt liquidation of each bank whose license has expired. In situations where one or more statutory grounds for license revocation have been met, the bank regulator should nevertheless have authority to let a bank keep its license—for instance, when the infraction of the bank is relatively minor and license revocation would be an abuse of authority; when a bank is deemed too big to fail; or when, in a systemic banking crisis, a mindless application of the rules would lead to the wholesale closure of the banking system.

2. Authority to Revoke the Banking License

Usually, the banking law provides for revocation of the banking license upon request of the bank (or its owners or management),[369] or when the banking license has not been used to engage in banking activities for a certain period of time.[370] Normally, such request will be granted if the bank is deemed solvent and the proceeds of the bank's liquidation would be adequate to cover the bank's liabilities.[371] Hereinafter, only revocation of the banking license as a regulatory response to banking problems will be discussed.

The bank regulator is generally given exclusive authority to revoke the banking license. There are good reasons for doing so. As was dis-

---

[369] E.g., *Italy*: Article 80(2) of the Law of 1993 on Matters Concerning Banks and Credit; *Netherlands*: Article 15(1)(a) of the Law on Supervision of the Credit System.

[370] E.g., *France*: Article 19(1) of Law No. 84-46 on the Activities and Supervision of Credit Institutions.

[371] In *Australia*, Section 9A(1) of the Banking Act 1959 requires that the bank regulator is satisfied that the revocation would not be contrary to the national interest and the interests of depositors of the bank.

cussed before, a regime where an agency other than the bank regulator is responsible for revocation of the banking license tends to weaken accountability. And if that agency is a member of the political establishment,[372] the regime is exposed to risk of political pressure and interference. In some countries, the law attempts to compromise by requiring that a banking license be revoked only upon the recommendation of the bank regulator.[373] In practice, however, the problem is not that too many banking licenses are improperly revoked, but rather that too few banking licenses are revoked. Controlling the authority of the bank regulator to revoke the banking license by making it subject to the consent of another authority is equally objectionable. Although a regime of shared responsibility may be effective in countries with a strong tradition of political discipline, it is rarely effective in most other countries.

There are conditions, however, when the law makes revocation of the operating license of a bank *mandatory*, leaving no room for discretion on the part of the bank regulator. This may be the case, for instance, when it has been decided that the bank is to be liquidated. Thus, in *England*, the banking license must be revoked if a winding-up order has been made against the bank or a resolution has been passed for the bank's voluntary winding-up;[374] in other circumstances, including the making of an administration order in relation to the bank under general insolvency law, revocation of the banking license is optional,[375] because the bank might yet be saved.

In some countries, the authority to revoke the banking license need not be exercised in cases where the bank is liquidated, regardless of the form such liquidation may take, when the bank is a corporation and its liquidation has the legal effect of dissolving the corporation.[376]

---

[372] An example is *Italy*, where banking licenses are revoked by the Minister of Finance, upon the recommendation of the Bank of Italy: Article 80(1) of the Law of 1993 on Matters of Banking and Credit.

[373] *Italy*: Article 80(1) of the Law of 1993 in Matters of Banking and Credit.

[374] Sections 11(6) and (9) of the Banking Act 1987. See for a similar provision *European Union*: Article 13(1) of the Amended Proposal for a Council Directive concerning the reorganization and the winding-up of credit institutions and deposit guarantee schemes (OJ No. C 36.8.2.1988, p. 1).

[375] E.g., Section 11(7) and (8) of the Banking Act 1987.

[376] E.g., in *Switzerland*: Merz and Raggenbass, "Switzerland," at p. 220.

3. Legal Effects of Revocation of the Banking License

The most obvious effect of the revocation of a bank's operating license is that, from the time that the revocation takes effect, the bank is no longer authorized to engage in core banking activities, such as receiving deposits from the public and using these to make loans.

In several countries, the law provides that if the banking license is revoked the bank must be liquidated or be wound up in bankruptcy.[377] Although there is a certain logic to such provisions, there are many activities engaged in by banks that are unregulated, do not require a banking license, and therefore are also carried out by nonbanks. This is particularly true for so-called universal banks offering securities and insurance brokerage services to the public. Why should corporations that lose their banking license not be permitted to continue engaging in unregulated activities that do not require a banking license? The former bank could continue its corporate life as a finance company. In *England*, the banking law does not require the liquidation of a bank when its banking license is revoked, even though the bank would be prohibited from engaging in regulated activities such as the acceptance of deposits. In other countries, the liquidation of a bank losing its banking license is optional under the law,[378] or the bank losing its banking license need only repay and liquidate deposits received from the public.[379]

---

[377] *Denmark*: Section 47(1) of the Law on Commercial Banks and Savings Banks; *Italy*: Article 80(1) of the Law of 1993 on Matters Concerning Banks and Credit; *Japan*: Article 40 of the Banking Law; *Norway*: Section 34 of the Law on Commercial Banks of 1961; *Switzerland*: Article 23quinquies of the Federal Law on Banks and Savings Banks.

[378] E.g., *Germany*: Section 38(1) of the Law on the Credit System.

[379] E.g., *France*: Article 19 of Law No. 84-46 on the Activities and Supervision of Credit Institutions; *Netherlands*: Article 15(5) of the Law on Supervision of the Credit System.

Principal Objectives To Be Pursued by Law

Unlike receivers, provisional administrators do not have the powers of bank owners. Therefore, provisional administrators must operate within the legal corporate structure of the bank to which they are appointed. Accordingly, provisional administration should be limited to those cases where it is expected that a bank in distress can be managed and operated back to regulatory compliance from within the institution or to conserve the value of the bank for its creditors pending its merger or liquidation. Provisional administration should be carried out in compliance with a clear plan of action adopted by the bank regulator, preferably in agreement with the bank's owners, and specifying detailed objectives of the administration.

The banking law should provide for a special receivership for banks supplementing the general insolvency regime, in order to provide an efficient system of restructuring and transfer of banking business where prompt action is required for compelling systemic reasons. The special bank receivership should be limited in scope and be carried out under judicial administration by the bank regulator or a trustee supervised by the bank regulator. The receivership provisions in the law could be modeled on principles of general insolvency law. The role of the judiciary in instituting and administering the bank receivership, and in protecting the interests of bank creditors and owners, can be calibrated to reflect the legitimate interests of the bank regulator, the need for efficiency, and the sociojuridical traditions of the country concerned.

The law should grant the bank regulator the exclusive authority to issue and to revoke the operating license of a bank. In principle, such authority should be discretionary.

XIII

Taking Control of a Bank Under General or Special Insolvency Law

1. General Issues

When viewed from a legal vantage point, the law of insolvency of banks is extraordinarily complex. General insolvency law—including both bankruptcy law and the law of reorganization by composition—is one of the most demanding fields of the law and this extends to the treatment of insolvent banks. In addition, whereas in many countries the general insolvency law is content to balance only three sets of competing interests, namely, the interests of creditors, owners, and employees, the law of bank insolvency addresses these and one more, namely, the interests of the public in a sound banking system, represented by the bank regulator. Subject to some important exceptions discussed below, the law governing the bankruptcy of banks is generally the same in a material sense as the general insolvency law that governs other enterprises. Therefore, a general reference is made to the extensive analysis of general insolvency law in the Insolvency Report of the Legal Department of the IMF; no attempt will be made to go over the same ground or to repeat its conclusions here.

In many countries (*Australia, Austria, Belgium, Denmark, England, France, Germany, Netherlands, Switzerland*), banks are subject to court-administered bankruptcy proceedings governed by general insolvency law.[380]

---

[380] *Australia*: Section 14F(2) of the Banking Act 1959 referring to the Corporations Law of a State or internal Territory under which the bank is incorporated, which includes the applicable provisions of general insolvency law; *Austria*: Article 82 of the Austrian Banking Act; *Belgium*: Article 29 of the Law on the Statute and Supervision of Credit Institutions; *England*: Section 92 of the Banking Act 1987; *France*: Article 3 of Law No. 85-98 on Bank Restructuring and Judicial Liquidation of Enterprises and *Court of Appeal of Paris*, March 2, 1990; D.1990.569, annotated by Vasseur; *Germany*: Section 46b of the Law on the Credit System; *Netherlands*: Article 77 of the Law on Supervision of the Credit System.

In some countries a special insolvency statute for banks replaces the general insolvency law.[381] Thus, in *Canada*, the Winding-up and Restructuring Act governs banks and also federally regulated trust and insurance companies, while general federal insolvency law governing corporations does not apply to banks:

> An interesting difference between the two regimes which illumi-
> nates the degree to which banks are regulated relative to other cor-
> porations is the principal process by which banks become subject to
> insolvency proceedings: (1) the threshold test for application of the
> insolvency regime to banks is not only insolvency but also other cri-
> teria related to the fitness of the bank to stay in business; (2) the
> instigator in the case of a bank is the regulator, while in the case of
> other corporations it is a creditor or someone with a financial inter-
> est in the corporation; and (3) to the extent that a control order in
> favour of the Superintendent of Financial Institutions is tantamount
> to the making of an insolvency order, the determination of insol-
> vency is made by a regulator in the exercise of his or her discretion
> rather than the courts, as is the case for other corporations.[382]

In some of the countries where the general insolvency law applies to banks, it is the only law governing bank receivership, and bank receiverships are formal judicial insolvency proceedings (*Australia, Austria, Belgium, England, Germany*). Rehabilitation procedures included in the general insolvency law may fulfill functions similar to the bank restructuring procedures of provisional administration or receivership under the banking law. For example, in *England*, under general insolvency law, the court may make an administration order in relation to a company, placing the company under the management of an administrator, if the court is satisfied that the company is or is likely to become unable to pay its debts, and considers that the making of an order would be likely to achieve one or more of the following purposes:

> the survival of the company, and the whole or any part of its
> undertaking, as a going concern;
>
> the approval or sanctioning of a compromise or other voluntary
> arrangement between the company and its creditors; and
>
> a more advantageous realization of the company's assets than
> would be effected on a winding up.[383]

---

[381] This treatment is distinguished from the cases where a more or less complete insolvency regime for banks is included in the banking law (*United States*), even though from a substantive point of view this distinction may appear somewhat artificial.

[382] Duffy, "Canada," at p. 36, footnote 10.

[383] Section 8 of the Insolvency Act 1986.

In *France*, general insolvency law authorizes the courts to take control of a bank in distress with the advice of the bank regulator.[384] One purpose served thereby is to rescue the bank as a going concern. An important feature of the French legislation is that the initiative for corrective action rests largely with the court. Thus, for instance, the law authorizes the President of the Commercial Court to call meetings with the management of a bank in distress and interested third parties, to gather information about the bank's condition from the bank and from monetary authorities, and to promote the formulation and adoption of a financing plan designed to correct the bank's problems; ultimately, if such financing plan cannot be adopted, the President of the Commercial Court may appoint a provisional administrator or may attempt to reach an arrangement with the bank's creditors suitable to ensure the continued operation of the bank.[385]

In the countries, such as *France*, where banks may be submitted to both regulatory administration under the banking law and a formal bankruptcy proceeding under insolvency law, it is possible that, while a bank is already under administration, a petition is filed with the court for bankruptcy of the bank and that general insolvency proceedings are opened against the bank. The effect of this may be that the existing administration is superseded by a bankruptcy proceeding. Alternatively, the existing administration continues as a regulatory receivership under a stricter application of the provisions of general insolvency law, to the extent that the general insolvency law did not already apply to the liquidation,[386] or the administration turns into a bankruptcy proceeding under the general insolvency law with the administrator continuing as bankruptcy receiver.[387] In *Australia*, the banking law takes precedence: while the bank regulator has control of

---

[384] Pursuant to Law No. 84-148 on the Prevention and Amicable Resolution of Difficulties of Enterprises, and Law No. 85-98 on the Judicial Rehabilitation and Liquidation of Enterprises; the advice of the regulator is required by Article 46-3 of Law No. 84-46 on the Activities and Supervision of Credit Institutions. In France, the banking law also authorizes provisional administration and receivership: Articles 44 and 46 of Law No. 84-46.

[385] Articles 34–36 of Law No. 84-148 on the Prevention and Amicable Settlement of Difficulties of Enterprises; Grenouilloux and Fernandez-Bollo, "France," at p. 57.

[386] The somewhat unusual statement in the last part of this sentence can be found in *the Netherlands*: Article 77(d) of the Law on Supervision of the Credit System.

[387] *Switzerland*: Articles 35(2) and (3) of the Federal Law on Banks and Savings Banks.

a bank's business, no external administrator must be appointed, whether under general insolvency law or corporation law.[388]

In *Switzerland*, general insolvency proceedings against a bank that is not overindebted are suspended by a judicial moratorium intended to achieve an extrajudicial rehabilitation of the bank, while the bank continues its banking activities under the supervision of a court appointed provisional administrator.[389]

2. Special Bank-Related Features of the General Insolvency Law

In countries where banks can be subject to a bankruptcy proceeding, the general insolvency law often gives recognition to the special status of banks and the role of the bank regulator.

Petitions

The parties entitled to bring a petition for bankruptcy of a bank would normally include the bank regulator, the bank, and the bank's creditors.[390]

In some countries, the law grants the regulator the exclusive right to petition for bankruptcy, to the exclusion of all other petitioners.[391] For banks under provisional administration, this right may be given to the provisional administrator.[392] It has been argued that this exclusive power serves to exclude frivolous bankruptcy petitions by creditors that could threaten the bank. However, frivolous petitions can be precluded by including a bankruptcy petition threshold in the law, for instance, by requiring that petitions are supported by overdue claims on the bank that total a specified minimum percentage of the bank's liabilities.

---

[388] Section 15A(2) of the Banking Act 1959. The law also provides that the appointment of an external administrator of a bank is terminated when the bank regulator takes control of a bank's business; Section 15A(1).

[389] Article 29(1ter) of the Federal Law on Banks and Savings Banks. See also Merz and Raggenbass, "Switzerland," p. 213 at pp. 221–22.

[390] See, e.g., *England*: Section 92 of the Banking Act 1987.

[391] *Denmark*: Article 47d(1) of the Consolidated Law on Commercial Banks and Savings Banks; *Germany*: Section 46b of the Law on the Credit System. Cf. *Austria*: Article 82(3) of the Austrian Banking Act, which provides that "normally" only the bank regulator may file for the institution of bankruptcy proceedings against a bank.

[392] *Austria*: Article 82(3) of the Austrian Banking Act; *Switzerland*: Article 35(2) of the Federal Law on Banks and Savings Banks, where the administrator brings the petition upon the instruction of the court.

Sometimes, the law makes the filing of a petition for bankruptcy of a bank mandatory. Examples would be the case where the bank becomes insolvent,[393] or where bank administration fails and the bank has become insolvent,[394] or where the bank cannot be rescued by bank administration within the time limit set by the law.[395]

The law often provides for participation of the bank regulator in general insolvency proceedings for a bank. Thus, for instance, the law may require the court to consult the bank regulator, before ruling on a petition for bankruptcy of a bank that is presented by another party.[396] In addition, the law may provide for participation of the bank regulator in the appointment of trustees, in meetings with creditors, or in the assessment of the bank's financial statements.[397]

It was argued before that there are significant policy-related costs attached to submitting bank receivership to judicial general insolvency proceedings. The most important of these costs concerns the risk that a judiciary that is not qualified to assess the interests of the banking system would nevertheless have the power to commence insolvency procedures against a bank that the monetary authorities have decided to rescue for systemic reasons.[398] To reduce this risk in countries where, notwithstanding this argument, it is decided to submit insolvent banks to receivership under the general insolvency law, it is suggested that the law of these countries be amended to provide that no general insolvency proceedings may be opened against a bank without the explicit consent of the central bank—representing the monetary authorities—and that such consent may be withheld only for systemic reasons. As such a provision would disregard the interests of bank creditors, the law may include the qualification that, before a bank may be so released from general insolvency proceedings, the central bank must show in court that the monetary authorities have determined that the business of the bank must be rescued as a going concern for systemic reasons, and that exceptional financial support is available to cover the bank's liabilities.

---

[393] *Denmark*: Article 47d(1) of the Consolidated Law on Commercial Banks and Savings Banks.

[394] *Switzerland*: Article 35(2) of the Federal Law on Banks and Savings Banks.

[395] *Canada*: Section 652 of the Bank Act and Section 39.22 of the Canada Deposit Insurance Corporation Act.

[396] *France*: Article 46-3 of Law No. 84-46 on the Activities and Supervision of Credit Institutions; *Netherlands*: Article 70 of the Law on Supervision of the Credit System.

[397] *Denmark*: Article 47d(2) and (3) of the Consolidated Commercial Bank and Savings Bank Act of 1991.

[398] See for a discussion of this issue Chapter VIII, Section 4, above.

Effects of the Opening of Insolvency Proceedings on Payment Systems

Many of the payments and securities transfers made by banks for their own account or for the account of their customers are processed by clearing and settlement systems. Often, such systems use net settlement procedures whereby payments or transfers between a bank and its counterparties in the system are periodically processed and netted against each other, producing a single net balance due to or from each participant.

Insolvency law typically provides that, from the time that insolvency proceedings are effectively opened by a court decision against a company, that company may no longer dispose of its assets. As payments and transfers are acts of disposal of assets, they are covered by such provisions. Orders for such payments and transfers are covered as well, and not only when they are issued after insolvency proceedings are opened, but also when they are issued to, but not yet fully executed by, a payment system before insolvency proceedings are opened. Consequently, payments or transfers whose execution is completed after insolvency proceedings are opened may be void or voidable by law.

To determine the legal effects of the opening of insolvency proceedings on particular payment or transfer orders that straddle the time that insolvency proceedings are opened, it is important to know precisely at what time the court decision opening the insolvency proceedings and the resulting statutory payment or transfer prohibition take effect.

Traditionally, a court decision opening insolvency proceedings and the resulting statutory prohibition on the disposal of assets take effect at the beginning of the day on which the decision is taken. This means that payments made during that day are void or voidable under the law.

Often, when a court decides to open an insolvency proceeding against a bank and a payment prohibition takes effect, payment and transfer orders issued by the bank are being processed at home and abroad by payment and transfer system operators who are blissfully ignorant of the court decision. Following the traditional rule giving effect to the court decision at the beginning of the day that it is rendered may force the operators to reverse on a subsequent day transactions that were processed for the bank during the previous day. Such reversals can be an administrative and operational nightmare, requiring the recalculation and resettlement of net balances due to or from the bank (and many other financial institutions that are counterparties of the bank), if these balances result from netting payments or transfers due to and from the bank concerned. Such reversals can cause gridlock and significantly slow down or suspend the operations of a payment or transfer system, with the potential of causing serious damage to the national economies concerned. It is not difficult to imagine that such reversals could ultimately constitute a major risk for the international monetary system, especially if they would concern a large clearing and net settlement system in a major international financial center, such as CHIPS in New York. Therefore, the effective time of a prohibition on executing a bank's payments and transfers, and the timely notification of that prohibition to payment and transfer systems operators, is of crucial importance to clearing and settlement systems.

There are several solutions to this problem, including the following.

In order to mitigate the risks inherent in the traditional effectiveness rule, at least one country has amended its legislation to provide that a court order opening insolvency proceedings against a bank, and its attendant prohibition on discharging the bank's obligations, will take effect at the beginning of the day *following* the day of the court order.[399]

According to the general insolvency law of *Switzerland*, bankruptcy proceedings against a bank are opened by court decision at the time specified in the decision, and any acts whereby the bank disposes of assets of its estate after that time are null and void with regard to the bank's creditors.[400] The following procedure has been adopted that permits the Swiss bank regulator to avoid problems for payment system operators that might otherwise result from these provisions of the insolvency law. When a bank's license is revoked, the bank is ordered by the regulator to cease business operations from a particular date and hour onwards determined by the regulator. The bank regulator can preempt problems for payment and transfer systems operators at home and abroad by (1) revoking a bank's license well before bankruptcy proceedings are opened against the bank; (2) specifying a time for the cessation of the bank's business operations that precedes the time that bankruptcy proceedings are opened against the bank; and (3) giving the payment and transfer systems operators advance notice of the time at which the bank must cease its business operations.[401]

---

[399] *Austria*: Article 2 of the Bankruptcy Code; and Thomas Wagner, and Birgit Sauerzopf, "Austria," in *International Bank Insolvencies: A Central Bank's Perspective*, ed. by Mario Giovanoli and Gregor Heinrich (The Hague: Kluwer Law International), 1999, at p. 23.

[400] Articles 175(1) and 204(1) of the Federal Debt Enforcement and Bankruptcy Law.

[401] See for a discussion of this technique Merz and Raggenbass, "Switzerland," p. 213 at pp. 217–18.

The most straightforward solution to the problem is for the law specifically to exempt payment and transfer system orders straddling the commencement of insolvency proceedings from the before-mentioned legal effects. This is the approach followed by the *European Union* Directive on settlement finality in payment and securities settlement systems.[402] The Directive establishes the following principles, which are to be incorporated into the national legislation of the member countries. Transfer orders entered into a payment or securities settlement system before the moment that the decision opening insolvency procedures is handed down shall be legally enforceable and be binding on third parties; transfer orders entered into such a system after the moment that the decision opening insolvency procedures is handed down and carried out on the day of opening of such proceedings shall be legally enforceable and binding on third parties only if, after the time of settlement, the settlement agent, the central counterparty, or the clearinghouse can prove that they were not aware, nor should have been aware, of the opening of such proceedings. Decisions opening insolvency proceedings shall immediately be notified to the authorities of the other member states. No law, regulation, rule, or practice on the setting aside of contracts and transactions concluded before the moment of opening of insolvency proceedings shall lead to the unwinding of a netting. The moment of entry of a transfer order into a system shall be defined by the rules of that system. Transfer orders entered into a system may not be revoked by a participant in the system or a third party from the moment defined by the rules of that system. Insolvency proceedings shall not have retroactive effects on the rights and obligations of a participant arising from, or in connection with, its participation in a system earlier than the moment of opening of such proceedings; these rights and obligations shall be determined by the law governing that system.[403]

---

[402] Directive 98/26/EC of the European Parliament and of the Council of 19 May 1998, *Official Journal L* 166, November 6, 1998, p. 45.

[403] The Directive is made effective at the national level by converting its rules into domestic law. As the text of the Directive is rather lengthy, some member states of the European Union have condensed it into shorter provisions of domestic law. However, statutory condensation is a hazardous enterprise. E.g., the statutory provisions adopted by *France* (Article 93-1 of Law No. 84-46 on the Activities and Supervision of Credit Institutions) and by the *Netherlands* (Article 71(9) and (10) of the Law on Supervision of the Credit System, amended by Law of December 17, 1998) differ both materially from the text of the Directive, and from each other.

Compositions

Some laws exclude composition proceedings and compositions with creditors with respect to banks.[404] The reasons may include that compositions are generally predicated on an assumption that the bank will be rehabilitated, an assumption that cannot be realized without consent of the bank regulator. Other countries do permit compositions, provided that they are approved by the bank regulator and the court.[405] In *Switzerland*, where compositions are permitted, the banking law provides that the receiver in bankruptcy of a bank exercises the powers of the meeting of the bank's creditors; this means that, even though creditor committees can be formed, the receiver must approve the schedule of claims and agree on the terms and conditions of a settlement.[406]

Setoff and Netting

Another technique to reduce the risks of bank failure for payment systems is to reduce the use banks make of payment systems.

A growing portion of a bank's business is with other banks (including nonbank financial institutions). Frequently, this business is conducted within the framework of long-term business relationships. Much of this business takes the form of spot transactions, swaps, options, and forward foreign exchange and interest rate transactions that banks conclude for their own account and risk or for the risk of their customers with other banks, requiring both parties to those transactions to exchange payments.

These exchanges of payments can be harnessed in a series of bilateral arrangements, one arrangement for each bank and each of its bank counterparties, in order to offset or otherwise net out the mutual rights and obligations of each pair of banks, so that the mutual debt exposure at any time for each pair of banks is reduced to a single net balance payable by one bank to the other. Such arrangements often take the form of a so-called master agreement covering specified categories of financial transactions; they specify the terms and conditions for the netting and settlement of the payments between the two banks resulting from individual transactions and they provide rules for contract

---

[404] *Austria*: Article 82(1) of the Austrian Banking Act.

[405] *Italy*: Articles 93 ff. of the Law of 1993 on Matters of Banking and Credit.

[406] Article 36(2) of the Federal Law on Banks and Savings Banks. See also Merz and Raggenbass, "Switzerland," p. 213 at p. 217.

termination and close-out netting in the event of a default or bankruptcy of one of the banks.

A major advantage of these arrangements is that they reduce the risk of default to payment systems, by converting what otherwise would have been two streams of payments between the two banks to one single net payment of one bank to the other. It is easy to see that this reduces the risk to a payment system of failure of one of the banks from a large number of payments for a large aggregate amount to a single net payment of a much smaller amount.

Reduction of risks of payment systems is not the only advantage of these arrangements. They also reduce the mutual exposure of banks to each other. Consequently, setoff and netting arrangements play an important role in curtailing the risk of international financial contagion, whereby domestic financial problems spread around the world through the failure of banks to meet their commitments to foreign banks, causing difficulties in turn for the foreign institutions and the foreign payment and transfer systems through which these commitments are to be settled.

The law of setoff usually provides that mutual obligations that are simultaneously due and payable are discharged *ipso facto*. Consequently, mutual debts between two banks that become due and payable and are therefore discharged by setoff *before* insolvency proceedings are opened against one of the banks would normally not be covered by the insolvency proceedings. However, the beforementioned master agreements between financial institutions often go beyond the general rule of setoff and also net out, under close-out netting covenants, payment obligations that would have become due and payable *after* the opening of insolvency proceedings against one of the institutions.

This raises the issue whether such extended close-out netting arrangements can be upheld in the event of bankruptcy or whether, pursuant to general principles of insolvency law, each leg of such mutual obligations would be disconnected from the other in order to run separately to and from the estate. The issue is of practical significance, as without close-out netting the creditors of insolvent banks would have to pay the full amount of their debt to the estate while they would usually receive only a fraction of their claim from the estate. Conversely, if close-out netting arrangements would be immune from the legal effects of insolvency, the creditor would be permitted to net out the full amount of his claim against the amount of his obligation to the estate, leaving only a net balance due to or from the estate.

Obviously, such immunity must be granted by an amendment of the insolvency law. Several countries have adopted such an amendment. Their legislation now provides that such close-out netting is exempt from the effects of insolvency proceedings.[407] These provisions have been included in banking law,[408] in general insolvency law,[409] in other general legislation,[410] or in a special statute.[411]

Although these provisions afford protection to payment and banking systems, they do so at the price of creating a special class of preference for claims of creditor banks and other financial institutions over the claims of other types of creditors. While financial creditors benefiting from netting agreements may use the full aggregate amount of their claims on an insolvent bank to reduce their obligations to the insolvency estate, other creditors with obligations to an insolvent bank that are matched by claims on the insolvency estate must pay their obligations in full when due, whereas they may expect only partial payment on their claims from the bank's estate on some distant future date. The ensuing inequality of treatment between financial and non-financial creditors of failing banks can be justified only by systemic risks that otherwise would be uncovered, and then only to the extent of what is required to cover those risks.

---

[407] The countries that have adopted such legislation include *Australia, Austria, Belgium, Canada, France, Germany, Luxembourg, Norway, Switzerland* and the *United States*. See the country reports in Giovanoli and Heinrich, eds., *International Bank Insolvencies*. See, for the *United States*, Joyce M. Hansen, and Nikki M. Poulos, "Treatment of Financial Contracts in Financial Institutions Insolvency," in *Bank Failures and Bank Insolvency Law in Economies in Transition*, ed. by Rosa M. Lastra and Henry N. Schiffman (The Hague: Kluwer Law International), 1999, Chapter 6.

[408] E.g., *France*: Article 93-2 of Law No. 84-46 on the Activities and Supervision of Credit Institutions.

[409] E.g., *Switzerland*: Article 211 of the Federal Debt Enforcement and Bankruptcy Law.

[410] E.g., *Norway*: Chapter 10 of the Securities Trading Act of 1997.

[411] E.g., *Australia*: the Payment System and Netting Act 1998; *Canada*: the Payment Clearing and Settlement Act.

Principal Objectives To Be Pursued by Law

If banks are submitted to general insolvency procedures, the special interests of the banking system must be served in the form of special provisions, such as provisions requiring consent of or consultation with the bank regulator before the court decides on a petition for bankruptcy of a bank. General insolvency proceedings must not be opened against a bank if the central bank determines that the bank should be rescued for systemic reasons and shows that the funds required to cover the bank's liabilities are available.

In countries where the law submits banks to both a special receivership or liquidation procedure under the banking law and a general insolvency procedure under other legislation, the law should delineate the scope of operation of these laws with respect to each other and provide for a more or less seamless transition from one procedure to the other.

Laws permitting setoff and netting of financial claims should be carefully weighed in light of the inequality of treatment they cause for nonfinancial institutions that are creditors of failing banks; they should be strictly limited to what is necessary to afford the required degree of protection against systemic risks.

XIV

Banking System Restructuring

1. Overview

Once a systemic banking crisis[412] occurs, the monetary authorities must act quickly and decisively to contain the crisis and its effects on the national economy. A systemic banking crisis generally requires measures that address not only the banking system itself but also the root causes and the effects of the crisis outside the banking sector. Thus, for instance, the authorities will not only try to contain the crisis by restoring public confidence in the banking system and to preserve a minimum of essential banking services, including measures to compensate for the sharp contraction in bank credit that typically follows a banking crisis, but will also take steps to protect other parts of the financial sector, such as the capital markets, and payment and securities transfer systems.

Restoring public confidence in the banking system, at home and abroad, is one of the most urgent and daunting tasks facing the monetary authorities. The recent history of banking crises in the United States, Latin America, Scandinavia, and East Asia teach that usually, to be successful, a response to a systemic banking crisis must include the following key elements.[413]

---

[412] In this book, a systemic banking crisis means the insolvency or threatened insolvency of so many banks in a country that the country's entire banking system, or an important sector of the banking system (savings and loan institutions), is threatened with collapse.

[413] See for extensive discussions of this topic: Federal Deposit Insurance Corporation, *History of the Eighties, Lessons for the Future—An Examination of the Banking Crises of the 1980s and Early 1990s*, FDIC, 1997. Also see the following published by the International Monetary Fund, Washington: Alicia García-Herrero, "Banking Crises in Latin America in the 1990s: Lessons from Argentina, Paraguay, and Venezuela," IMF Working Paper 97/140, 1997; Claudia Dziobek, and Ceyla Pazarbaşoğliu, "Lessons from Systemic Bank Restructuring: A Survey of 24 Countries," IMF Working Paper 97/161, 1997; Burkhard Drees, and Ceyla Pazarbaşoğliu, *The Nordic Banking Crises—Pitfalls in Financial Liberalization*, IMF Occasional Paper No.161, 1998; Carl-Johan Lindgren, and others, *Financial Sector Crisis and Restructuring—Lessons from Asia*, IMF Occasional Paper No. 188, 1999; and Gillian Garcia, "Deposit Insurance and Crisis Management," IMF Working Paper 00/57, 2000.

167

An interagency bank crisis team should be appointed to prepare a comprehensive bank restructuring program for adoption by the political establishment and to coordinate execution of the program among the various agencies concerned, such as the bank regulator, the deposit insurance agency, the central bank, and the ministries of finance, treasury, and economic affairs. It is preferable to entrust bank restructuring to an interagency team. Usually the effects of a systemic banking crisis extend well beyond the banking system. In a national economic crisis, the restructuring of the banking sector will largely depend on the ability of the domestic corporate sector to meet its liabilities toward the banks, and may well require corporate sector reform. Finally, the operational and financial assistance needed for the rehabilitation of the banking sector exceeds the capacities of the bank regulator, usually demands significant fiscal outlays and far-reaching structural reforms of the regulatory and legal frameworks in which banks operate, and therefore requires the firm support of the political establishment.

Recent analyses of banking crises in the 1990s show that the probability of success of a bank restructuring program is improved and the negative macroeconomic impact of a banking crisis is reduced if, from the beginning, the program is conceived and presented to the public as a consistent and comprehensive strategy; programs that developed in a piecemeal fashion over time were deemed less successful.[414]

A bank restructuring program should detail macroeconomic and financial policies and measures designed to contain the crisis and to restore viability to the banking system. It should accompany and be consistent with a credible macroeconomic stabilization program with comprehensive financial sector restructuring and reform strategies. A bank restructuring program should provide appropriate incentives to all economic agents concerned (depositors and other bank creditors, bank owners, borrowers, and bank administrators) in order to promote the restructuring process, to reduce moral hazard, and to minimize the cost of bank restructuring to the government. Adoption and execution of a bank restructuring program should be marked by prompt publication of the program and its revisions, and by frequent disclosure of all

---

[414] Good examples of successful comprehensive bank restructuring programs are found in *Sweden, Argentina,* and *Korea*; examples of countries where a less decisive and fragmented response created problems are *Venezuela* and *Indonesia*. See García-Herrero, "Banking Crises in Latin America in the 1990s," at pp.11–12. See in general for Sweden and the Asian countries, respectively: Drees and Pazarbaşioğlu, *The Nordic Banking Crises,* and Lindgren and others, *Financial Sector Crisis and Restructuring.*

significant information concerning the restructuring process to interested parties, both at home and abroad.

Bank restructuring is nearly always required in order to avoid that insolvent institutions would continue to operate and thereby worsen the crisis by contributing to distortions in economic incentives and moral hazard. Taking control of insolvent banks is typically needed to facilitate debt workouts and the resumption of capital flows, and to minimize fiscal costs and monetary policy constraints. Structural reforms may be required to address public concerns that fundamental flaws in the banking system contributed to the crisis. Often reforms cannot be limited to the institutional, administrative, and legal framework in which banks conduct their activities, but must extend beyond the banking system to correct structural deficiencies in the corporate sector (*Korea*) or even the sociopolitical regime (*Indonesia*).

In the five countries most affected by the Asian crisis of 1997,[415] extensive liquidity support was provided by the central bank. Such support must usually be sterilized by monetary policy operations, even though a central bank's ability to engage in open-market operations may be constrained by the crisis. An added bonus of open-market operations is that they can help in redistributing liquidity from banks with increasing deposits to banks losing deposits and credit lines.[416] In countries whose law excludes central bank liquidity support to banks that are deemed insolvent, financial assistance must be provided by the government.[417]

Among the most serious conditions accompanying a systemic banking crisis is the loss of confidence in the local economy on the part of foreign exchange traders and foreign financial institutions. Foreign exchange reserves and foreign trade credit lines must be protected. Foreign investors must be dissuaded from liquidating their local investments. Especially foreign banks must be persuaded to keep their local branch offices open, as the implicit home office guarantee of their liabilities may attract domestic deposits and thus exert a stabilizing influence on the deposit base.[418] Foreign exchange speculators must be denied access to local currency loans and derivative instruments used for sales of the national currency in the foreign exchange

---

[415] *Indonesia, Korea, Malaysia,* the *Philippines,* and *Thailand.*

[416] Lindberg and others, *Financial Sector Crisis and Restructuring,* at p. 18.

[417] See Chapter VI, above.

[418] This was the case, e.g., in *Argentina* and *Paraguay:* García-Herrero, "Banking Crises in Latin America in the 1990s," at p. 10.

markets. Therefore, capital outflows may have to be curtailed by capital controls[419] and debt-rescheduling arrangements may have to be negotiated.

Many countries faced by a systemic banking crisis during the last two decennia have resorted to issuing a *blanket guarantee* protecting depositors and other creditors of banks.[420] To be accepted by the public and to stem runs on the banks, a blanket government guarantee must be credible. The credibility of the guarantee can be enhanced by various measures. For instance, blanket government guarantees issued by Asian countries during the crisis of 1997 were strengthened by making the terms of the guarantee explicit, by issuing the guarantee in the form of a law or decree, and by making the guarantee part of a comprehensive restructuring strategy and the country's macroeconomic program.[421] The moral hazard inherent in such guarantees may be reduced by limiting the time during which the guarantee will be in effect, as well as by denying bank owners free ridership by closing insolvent banks and imposing guarantee fees on solvent banks, even though it is notoriously difficult to find a proper price for such guarantees.

In a systemic banking crisis, insolvent banks should be closed expeditiously. Among the advantages of closing insolvent banks are the elimination of further losses and moral hazard, and the termination of official liquidity support. However, the closure of a significant part of a national banking system carries major costs; these include the resulting systemic reduction in banking services, such as domestic credit lines and the intermediation of payments and securities transfers, as well as the risk that bank closings fuel panic runs on other banks, although this risk can be alleviated by a credible blanket guarantee from the government.[422]

If the closure of all insolvent banks would lead to the extinction of the banking system, for instance, because the country has only several

---

[419] During the Asian crisis of 1997, *Indonesia, Malaysia,* the *Philippines,* and *Thailand* all imposed some capital restrictions on foreign residents; those imposed by Malaysia were the most extensive. See, for a description of the restrictions, Lindgren and others, *Financial Sector Crisis and Restructuring,* Box 6 at p. 20.

[420] See, for an extensive analysis of the issuance of blanket guarantees for deposits and other liabilities of banks during a systemic banking crisis, Garcia, "Deposit Insurance and Crisis Management," at pp. 52–71. Blanket guarantees were issued by the governments of *Finland, Indonesia, Jamaica, Japan, Korea, Kuwait, Malaysia, Mexico, Sweden, Thailand,* and *Turkey, ibid.,* at p. 67.

[421] Lindgren, and others, *Financial Sector Crisis and Restructuring,* at p. 20.

[422] See, for the experience in Asia, *ibid.,* at pp. 21–23.

large banks all of which are insolvent, other solutions must be found. These may consist of open-bank assistance by the monetary authorities, preferably under provisional administration including nationalization of the banks in whole or in part by the government (while any remaining part of the bank would be liquidated).[423]

The law may offer special instruments designed to combat a banking crisis. For instance, in *Germany*, the banking law authorizes the federal government by regulation to establish a *moratorium* for any bank when a banking crisis threatens, namely, if there is reason to fear that banks may encounter financial difficulties that warrant expectations of grave danger to the national economy and particularly to the orderly functioning of general payments; the law extends the protection of the moratorium beyond debt service to other transactions of the bank, and provides that no execution, attachment, or foreclosure can be carried out or completed concerning bank assets protected by the moratorium.[424] As was suggested before,[425] it is difficult to understand how banks placed under such a moratorium could continue their operations, and it must be considered doubtful whether a general suspension of payments can do much to maintain or to restore confidence in the banking system. For these reasons, during a banking system crisis, a moratorium, though useful for insolvent banks placed in receivership pending their liquidation or merger with another institution, might be counterproductive for banks that are still viable and that need to continue their operations as normally as possible in order to provide indispensable banking services. Compared with a moratorium, a blanket guarantee appears to be preferable because it is designed to promote confidence in the banking system by ensuring payment of bank liabilities and to support the national economy by ensuring the continued more or less normal operation of viable banks.

2. Institutional and Functional Features

Absent a banking crisis, the bank regulator is usually in charge of administering the corrective measures indicated when banks become illiquid or insolvent. Although staff and budgetary resources available to a bank-supervision agency are usually adequate to discharge this

---

[423] See, for the use of these strategies in *Norway* and *Sweden*, Drees and Pazarbaşioğlu, *The Nordic Banking Crises*, at pp. 26–31.

[424] *Germany*: Section 47(1) of the Law on the Credit System.

[425] See Chapter VII, above.

function on an incidental basis, they are rapidly overwhelmed by a full-blown systemic banking crisis, threatening its ability to continue prudential supervision of the banks that remained more or less healthy.[426]

Often, the financial structure of the bank regulator is ill-suited to carry out the task of reorganizing a significant part of a banking system. Usually, the regulator cannot bear the costs of such reorganization from its own resources, not even if it is the central bank. And, if the central bank is the bank regulator, it is often not authorized to extend financial assistance to banks that are insolvent, or to receive budgetary funds for its own account other than in the form of equity capital; moreover, it may well be regarded as improper for a central bank to do all the commercial activities required in a banking system reorganization for its own account and on its own books. If the regulator is constituted as a commission without legal personality, it may lack the legal and financial robustness required for the task and its funding.

In some countries, the deposit insurance agency is designated by law to take the lead role in the bank restructuring process.[427] As was explained before,[428] this role of the deposit insurance agency is bound to create conflicts between its interests as a major bank creditor and its fiduciary duties as an impartial administrator of bank resolution procedures. Another problem is that, usually, the funding of the deposit insurance agency is insufficient for the task; as is common for other types of insurance funds, deposit insurance is normally not funded to cover the risk of a universal disaster in the form of massive defaults on deposit liabilities of banks. Therefore, in most systemic banking crises where there is deposit insurance, the deposit insurance fund will have to be recapitalized, sometimes more than once, requiring significant fiscal outlays. It is the hope that such outlays can be curtailed and that the banking system can be stabilized with a minimum of demand on the deposit insurance fund that drives governments into issuing blanket guarantees to depositors and other bank creditors.

Typically, the reconstruction of a banking sector demands more than the closing and liquidation of insolvent banks. It requires the consolidation of insolvent banks or parts of such banks into viable institutions that can serve the banking system. This endeavor extends

---

[426] This need not be the case in countries with few banking institutions.

[427] This is the case in the *United States.*

[428] See Chapter VIII, Section 3, above, for a brief discussion of this issue.

beyond the treatment of individual banks to the restructuring of the entire banking sector.

Therefore, often, systemic banking crises do not lend themselves to treatment in the general insolvency courts. If large numbers of bank failures are involved, the courts would be overwhelmed, especially when, as is often the case, the systemic banking crisis is accompanied by a general economic crisis causing massive failures in the corporate sector to be administered in the same insolvency courts. Also, a systemic and consolidated approach to bank restructuring cannot be reconciled with traditional judicial insolvency procedures designed to treat insolvent enterprises on an individual basis. This is an important reason for placing systemic bank restructuring outside the framework of general insolvency law. And, in a systemic banking crisis, the consideration that individual bank owners and creditors are thereby deprived of the protection afforded by a proper judicial insolvency proceeding is outweighed by the overriding national interest in restoring the banking system in the shortest possible time.

Bank Restructuring in Sweden

The successful strategy followed by Sweden during the banking crisis of the early 1990s may serve to illustrate the content and execution of a comprehensive bank restructuring program.[429]

One of the main components of the strategy was the blanket guarantee announced by the Swedish government in September 1992 to the effect that all bank commitments would be met on a timely basis and that no depositors, creditors, or other counterparties of banks would suffer any losses. The blanket guarantee received parliamentary ratification by the Bank Support Act of December 1992. Only share capital and perpetual debentures were excluded from the guarantee. The government was authorized to provide financial assistance in the form of loan guarantees, capital contributions, and other appropriate measures, without the constraint of an upper limit. The Bank Support Act of 1992 provided, *inter alia,* that support provided to banks in the form of payments should be recovered to the fullest extent possible, but that the government should not endeavor to assume ownership of banks. The blanket guarantee was considered to be exceptional and

---

[429] See in general, Stefan Ingves, and Göran Lind, "The Management of the Bank Crisis in Retrospect," *Quarterly Review,* Sveriges Riksbank, 1996, pp. 5–18; Drees and Pazarbaşioğlu, *The Nordic Banking Crises,* at p. 35.

temporary; it was repealed by parliament and replaced by a limited deposit insurance scheme in July 1996. In May 1993, a Bank Support Authority was formally established as an independent agency to manage the government support system.[430]

Other principles underlying the success of Sweden's bank restructuring strategy have been summarized as follows:[431]

> The key element of the restructuring program was the formation of a broad political consensus. This consensus was supported by timely information to all domestic parties. Transparency and disclosure of information were crucial for regaining confidence domestically and abroad; the implications of support measures for depositors and investors were extensively reported.

> It was decided that to place the lead restructuring agency within existing institutions, such as the Ministry of Finance or the Riksbank, might have interfered adversely with the roles of these institutions. Therefore, a separate institution—the Bank Support Authority—was created to implement the bank restructuring strategy. The formation of an institutional framework clarified the respective roles for the Ministry of Finance, the Riksbank, the Financial Supervisory Authority, and the Bank Support Authority. At the same time, there was a continuous exchange of information among the institutions.

> Diagnosis was the first step in the restructuring exercise. A common yardstick—based on the capital adequacy ratio and other financial ratios—was designed to measure the degree of problems in banks. Initially the banks were divided into two main categories: those that were considered viable and those that were not. While banks in the first category received support, the ones in the second category were closed or merged, and the banks' creditors were paid off.

> Distorted incentives were minimized through the conditionality measures embedded in support agreements. The foremost conditions included changing management and upgrades of internal control and risk-management systems (which in most cases were found to be inadequate). The parliamentary guarantee did not cover owners' capital; in case of financial support by the government, owners typically lost their equity stakes.

> Structural reforms of the accounting, legal, and regulatory framework and of prudential supervision were enacted. Clear guidelines on asset classification and valuation of banks' holdings of collateral (real estate and other assets) were set, with the Bank Support Authority monitoring compliance with these procedures.

---

[430] Drees and Pazarbaşioğlu, *The Nordic Banking Crises*, at p. 29.
[431] *Ibid.* at p. 35.

The establishment of institutions for loan workout was given high priority. Problem assets were transferred, at an assumed market price,[432] to a separate asset-management company. As with other types of support provided to the banks, strict conditionality was attached to these operations. This approach facilitated the orderly sale of assets and allowed problem banks to continue their usual business without having to handle a large volume of workout cases. The asset-management company could recruit the specific expertise needed for transforming the bad assets into salable assets. The Bank Support Authority funded the asset-management companies and was their sole owner.

Bank Restructuring Corporations

Several of the countries faced with a systemic banking crisis in recent years have established one or more separate state agencies to rehabilitate or to liquidate problem banks. The most common such agencies are bank restructuring corporations (BRCs).

The activities of a BRC should be defined and delineated in time and scope by the law establishing the BRC. For instance, a BRC may be created to handle a systemic crisis for a temporary period, typically five or more years. The law may prescribe a division of labor between the BRC and the deposit insurance agency based on the type of banking institution, or the nature of the task, i.e., bank restructuring versus asset management. In other cases, a BRC may be created to handle a more discrete problem, such as the restructuring and bank restructuring of insolvent state-owned banks.

The law establishing the BRC should specify the criteria to be used for identifying banks whose financial condition permits them to continue banking operations under the supervision of the bank regulator, banks that should be closed and liquidated outright, and banks whose financial condition or position in the banking system makes them eligible for bank restructuring. For the banks that fall in the last two categories, regulatory responsibility may be transferred from the bank regulator to the BRC. The law should provide that such a transfer must be publicly notified and has the effect of transferring complete control over the bank and its assets to the BRC.

The BRC will take immediate control of the banks transferred to it, and will secure their assets by removing them from the control of bank

---

[432] The key concern was to make sure that all potential losses were borne by banks rather than the asset-management companies.

managers and owners. The banks to be liquidated will be wound up; those of their assets that cannot immediately be sold will be kept or transferred to another entity (hospital bank or asset management entity) for management and future disposal.

Preferably, the law should require the BRC to carry out its bank restructuring activities in accordance with detailed bank restructuring plans, one for each bank brought under the jurisdiction of the BRC. The plans are formulated on the basis of an assessment by the BRC of the financial condition of the bank and the chances that the bank can be successfully restructured. These plans may be agreed upon between the BRC, the bank regulator, and the monetary authorities, so as to ensure their consistency with the country's overall bank restructuring program and budget constraints. They may periodically be revised and updated to reflect, *inter alia*, changes in the needs of the banking system and the condition of banks submitted to the bank restructuring process.

The goals of a BRC are to consolidate the banking system, to recapitalize viable banks, and to improve bank balance sheets by removing nonperforming assets. Consolidation may take a number of forms. Thus, BRCs typically restructure, liquidate, or sell problem banks, and manage, restructure, or sell assets of problem banks. They may use techniques for maximizing the going-concern value of banks—notably purchase and assumption transactions—that are similar to the resolution procedures used in a bank receivership. In one approach, two or more insolvent institutions under the BRC's jurisdiction are merged by the BRC into a new institution, which is then recapitalized with government funds. By so doing, larger and (at least in theory) more viable institutions are created that may later be reprivatized by selling stock back to the public. In a second approach, an insolvent bank is merged with a solvent bank that may be undercapitalized, which may then receive a capital infusion of government funds from the BRC. In either case, the BRC is sometimes able to recoup some of its costs from the sale of shares at a later date.

Recapitalization of an insolvent bank typically involves the infusion of new capital into the institution, with or without a merger or consolidation, with new management installed by the BRC running the bank until it may be reprivatized. Cleaning bank balance sheets may be accomplished by having the BRC or another entity purchase assets, hopefully at market values to avoid any subsidy that would result in a valuation based on book values; the assets may later be sold in a variety of transactions, including, but not limited to, bulk sales and asset securitization.

An often controversial policy issue is whether and how the BRC will provide financial assistance to acquirers of insolvent banks. In some cases, the BRC has the power to grant financial assistance to acquirers of banks, such as equity, loans, deposits, guarantees, or indemnities. It is often difficult to find acquirers of banks unless all nonperforming assets have been removed, and the balance sheet completely cleaned out. However, even in such cases, the threat of litigation from former owners, managers, and creditors can give rise to a contingent liability that acquirers will want to be protected against. In such cases, the ability of the BRC to provide a guarantee or indemnity may be a necessary aspect of the financial assistance that it can offer. The use of guarantees and indemnities may create contingent liabilities on the BRC's balance sheet that may linger far beyond the agency's role in the acquisition itself. The difficult question of who should bear the risk of loss may be resolved in different ways at different stages of a systemic crisis, depending on the demands of and the degree of competition between buyers of insolvent banks.

One of the thorniest problems encountered in a banking system crisis is that the establishment of reasonable values for many bank assets has become difficult. Nonperforming loan asset values are nearly impossible to assess as the impaired creditworthiness of many corporate borrowers rapidly deteriorates further. Collateral values are hard to determine as markets for those assets dry up. Valuations based on discounted present values become unreliable as the uncertainties concerning cash flows, interest rates, and other financial variables increase. Nevertheless, such valuations are usually necessary for banking institutions to asses their book value in order to determine whether they are insolvent and, if so, whether they meet the criteria for restructuring or outright liquidation. In addition, asset values drive choices between different restructuring strategies and ultimately help determine sales prices. A contributing problem is that this uncertain environment may produce dramatic differences in accounting results for similar asset classes, not only over time, but also simultaneously for different banks, as asset valuations increasingly come to depend on judgments that can honestly differ. Although this problem cannot be solved definitively, it can be reduced by establishing, by bank regulation, firm accounting rules, standards, and procedures that must be applied uniformly to all banks entering the restructuring process.[433]

---

[433] See, for a description of the experience gained from the Asian crisis of 1997, Lindgren and others, *Financial Sector Crisis and Restructuring*, at pp. 31–32.

Autonomy of BRCs

There is widespread agreement that, to be successful at these tasks, BRCs must have sufficient autonomy. The need for autonomy means mainly that the agencies should be created either as private corporations or as independent legal entities of the state, and that they should be operationally and financially separate and distinct from the political establishment and national monetary authorities, such as the central bank. Financial autonomy requires adequate funding of the agencies from reliable sources, such as the state budget, through loans from the deposit insurance agency, or from proceeds of sales of bank assets. Experience indicates that countries that have established an autonomous BRC generally have been more successful than those that have chosen not to endow it with sufficient independence.[434]

Among the reasons given why autonomy is a fundamental legal objective are the following. First, the cost of restructuring the banking sector during a time of financial crisis will be significant, necessitating direct appropriations as part of the budgetary process or funding from other sources, which requires the recipient BRC to have the corporate structure of an independent legal entity allowing it to receive, and to be independently accountable for the use of, such funds. Accordingly, systemic bank restructuring legislation typically establishes BRCs as independent legal bodies and makes explicit provision for funding that includes capitalization by the government and sometimes the authority to borrow from the central bank or the government, or to issue debt instruments that may or may not carry the full faith and credit of the state.

In addition, making a BRC part of, or effectively controlled by, the bank regulator, would give rise to real or perceived conflicts of interest based on differences in the roles played by the BRC and the regulator. The bank regulator should maintain an arm's-length relationship with the BRC, which typically operates and owns stock in insolvent banks while those banks may continue to be supervised by the bank regulator. Moreover, the bank regulator is not well situated to make the operational decisions required in managing a bank, liq-

---

[434] An example of successful autonomous bank restructuring corporations can be found in the *United States*, which organized the Resolution Trust Corporation (RTC) and the Federal Deposit Insurance Corporation (FDIC) as independent agencies of the government. These two institutions liquidated or sold over 2,000 banking institutions and more than $600 billion in assets during the period 1985–95 (the RTC was created in 1989).

uidating assets, or to decide on when and how to resolve a bank by sale, merger, or liquidation, or to issue stock to recapitalize or reprivatize a bank.

Finally, organizing a BRC as an autonomous entity helps to insulate and protect the rest of the government, including the central bank and the ministry of finance, from political shock waves that often follow the myriad difficult decisions that must be taken by the BRC. These include removing bank management, curtailing or overriding ownership interests, restructuring the bank's assets and liabilities, and managing, collecting, and liquidating problem assets. At the same time, the independence of the agency helps to insulate and protect it from political interference, as bank owners, depositors, and other creditors and borrowers seek to influence or overturn BRC decisions. The use of an independent board of directors, a majority of whom are not government ministers, typically has the effect of promoting and reinforcing the autonomy of bank restructuring corporations, as do stringent restrictions on the removal of board members that protect them from the political fallout of unpopular decisions.

The foregoing consideration should not be taken to exclude the bank regulator entirely from the bank restructuring process. The bank regulator and the BRC should consult each other regularly with respect to banks undergoing restructuring in order to facilitate their eventual reentry into the economy. The bank regulator retains primary responsibility for determining for each bank whether that bank should be transferred to the BRC for restructuring or liquidation and, once the bank has been restructured by the BRC, whether control of the bank should be returned to its owners.

There are countries, however, that would not admit the degree of autonomy needed by a BRC and where, therefore, a BRC would not be the most suitable instrument to restructure a banking sector. For example, a country may determine that a centralized BRC could not be endowed with the requisite autonomy from the political establishment or could not be properly staffed with qualified personnel. Such countries may elect instead to pursue a banking system restructuring plan that relies on the banks themselves to reorganize their financial condition. This may be done in accordance with debt workout procedures established for the purpose that cover not only bank debt but also nonperforming loan assets of banks; participation by the banks in the plan and their compliance with its requirements may be ensured by offering appropriate incentives to the banks, including financial support from the government.[435] Alternatively, the threat that the bank regulator will use its statutory authority to deprive owners of undercapitalized banks of their equity interest may be sufficient incentive for such owners actively to pursue the recapitalization or merger of their banks.[436]

3. Legal Aspects

To be effective, BRCs must be grounded in strong and well-conceived legislation whose underpinnings rest on principles of administrative law, including in particular transparency and proportionality. Often, this will include special banking system restructuring legislation establishing BRCs, setting rules for the transfer of banks to their jurisdiction and for the exit of banks, and governing the administration and operation of the BRCs.

Transparency

During a banking crisis, full public disclosure of the objectives pursued in rehabilitating the banking system and of the applicable institutional arrangements and rules of law is a prerequisite for restoring public confidence in the banking system. Therefore, the law governing the BRC and its activities must use clear, comprehensive, and unambiguous language and must be comprehensible to bank owners and management, potential investors in, and buyers of, restructured banks and their assets, and the public at large. The need for transparency is especially important in defining the grounds and procedures for referral and transfer of a failing bank to the BRC; the legal effects of the transfer of a bank to the BRC on the powers and rights of bank owners and managers with respect to the bank; the content and scope of the powers of the BRC; and the circumstances under which banks referred to the BRC must be liquidated and their licenses must be revoked. Also,

---

[435] This approach was followed successfully in *Poland* (1994–96) pursuant to the Law of February 2, 1993 on Financial Restructuring of Enterprises and Banks. An important advantage was that the banking system was dominated by a relatively small number of state and former state banks. See, in general, Monte-Negret, and Papi, *The Polish Experience with Bank and Enterprise Restructuring*, Policy Research Working Paper 1705 (Washington: World Bank), 1997.

[436] This technique appears to have worked in *Argentina*; see Danny M. Leipziger, "The Argentine Banking Crisis: Observations and Lessons," in *Preventing Banking Crises: Lessons from Recent Global Bank Failures*, ed. by Caprio, Hunter, Kaufman, and Leipziger, 1998 (Washington, World Bank), p. 35 at p. 41.

if the statute of a BRC grants rights, powers, and procedures that conflict with or override other laws, such as company law, bankruptcy law, securities law, real property law, and employment law, the hierarchy between the statute of the BRC and these other laws should be clearly stated in the organic law of the BRC.

Grounds for Referral of Banks

What grounds will be used by the bank regulator to refer a bank to the BRC? Typically, banks must be insolvent before they are referred to the BRC. The definition of insolvency should be clearly stated in the law, such as the failure of the bank to pay its obligations as they fall due. Balance sheet insolvency, based on liabilities being greater than assets, and regulatory insolvency, based on capital inadequacies, are also used. Additional criteria may be imposed, such as the size of a bank's deposit liabilities or loan assets, in order to limit the number of banks that are referred to the BRC.

Legal Effects of Referral of Banks

Based on the fact that it concerns a quasi-insolvency process, the referral of a bank to the BRC should be *ipso facto*, and for the duration of the restructuring process, vest the powers of all corporate organs of the bank in the BRC, and place the bank in a debt-service moratorium where enforcement actions by creditors against the bank are suspended, except perhaps for foreclosure on collateral. The law must be clear that, when a bank comes under the jurisdiction of the BRC, the BRC becomes solely responsible for the management and operation of the bank.

Another policy issue involves the legal status of the bank: will a bank remain open (i.e., will its banking license still be in place) while it is under BRC administration, or will the bank be closed as part of the restructuring process? The answer will in part depend on the question whether the bank should be rescued for systemic reasons or not.

Powers of the BRC

In serving the goal of transparency of public administration and legal certainty, the powers of the BRC should be explicitly stated in the law, with more rather than fewer listed. These powers should be established by statute, and not by decree as the latter are easily changed, contributing to uncertainty about the law. For the BRC, these powers typically include three levels of authority, starting with the BRC's authority as a juridical person, with all the powers flowing therefrom, such as the power to own and dispose of property, to sue and be sued, and to enter into and enforce contracts. The second level of BRC authority derives from the powers of the bank under administration, its owners and managers, such as the power to take deposits, to lend money, and to sell and restructure the bank and its assets and liabilities; it is based on a statutory provision that vests these powers in the BRC. The last level of authority is the so-called "superpowers" commonly granted to trustees or receivers under a bankruptcy regime, such as the power to stay litigation, to repudiate burdensome contracts, to transfer liabilities without creditor consent, and to reinstate contracts that have terminated based on a bankruptcy or insolvency clause.

An unusual power, which may be practically significant, that should be granted to the BRC is the power to charter new banks that could function as bridge banks in a purchase and assumption transaction or as permanent new banking institutions combining assets and liabilities of two or more closed banks.[437]

Proportionality

As the powers necessary for a successful banking system restructuring must typically be unusually extensive, care should be taken that the powers granted by law to the BRC are proportional to the agency's tasks. Although the serious consequences of a systemic banking crisis justify unusual restrictions on property rights, this justification does not support measures that are clearly excessive. This means that the scope of the powers of the agency should not extend beyond what is strictly necessary to discharge its tasks. In particular, the law should not contain an open-ended grant of authority to the BRC permitting it to create additional powers for itself or to expand its statutory powers through the issuance of regulations, decrees, or orders.

There are unfortunate instances where the principle of proportionality is flouted and a BRC is given excessive powers. One of these concerns the *Indonesian Bank Restructuring Agency* (IBRA). During the Asian crisis of 1997, IBRA was established with extensive powers listed in the banking law of Indonesia.[438] These powers were subsequently expand-

---

[437] See, for an example, *United States*: 12 U.S.C. § 1821(n).
[438] Article 37A of Law No. 7/1992 on Banking, as amended by Law No. 10/1998 of November 10, 1998.

ed by government regulation,[439] well beyond the scope of what was provided in the banking law. In particular, the government regulation authorized IBRA to determine *"the procedure needed to control, manage and undertake ownership measures concerning ... assets under restructuring,"* which were defined to include not only the assets owned by the insolvent banks administered by IBRA but also assets owned by the debtors of these banks.[440] The stated intent of this authority was to permit IBRA to force debtors of the banks under its administration to negotiate with IBRA in good faith. The draconian result was that IBRA, established under the banking law for the resolution of banks entrusted to its administration, could effectively control not only the restructuring of those banks but also indirectly the restructuring of all corporations that had debts to such banks, by threatening seizure of the assets of "uncooperative" corporations. Thus, IBRA could exercise control over much of the corporate sector of Indonesia. These excessive powers did little to give IBRA domestic and international credibility.

Rights of Bank Owners

Banking system restructuring generally requires the transfer to a BRC of all rights of owners in banks submitted to BRC jurisdiction. To be effective and efficient, banking system restructuring must override the safeguards afforded by the company law to shareholders; this is fully justified by the severity of a systemic banking crisis. Also, as in any bank restructuring, free ridership of existing bank owners must be avoided.

In some countries, the transfer of bank ownership to a government agency, such as a BRC, may raise questions as to its constitutionality. Where possible, these should be addressed by the law so as to avoid taxing an already overburdened judiciary and regulatory system by unnecessary litigation. However, the risk of successful litigation on the part of owners or managers of a bank transferred to a BRC should not be exaggerated. Given that the insolvent bank's share price at this point is usually at or around zero, and that the level of its capital is at zero or below, ownership interests, while legally valid, will have only a theoretical value in the marketplace. In other words, even if an owner

---

[439] Government Regulation No. 17 of 1999 on the Indonesian Bank Restructuring Agency.
[440] Articles 48 *juncto* 1 of Government Regulation 17 of 1999 and Article 7 of a Decree of the Chairman of IBRA issued on October 4, 1999.

could prove to a court that there has been a taking of property by the government in a manner contrary to law, the damages that could be proven and claimed would be *de minimis*.

Review of Administrative Acts

Normally, the agencies involved in banking system restructuring are government agencies and as such they and their acts are governed by administrative law, including procedures for administrative review. Because of the urgency and exceptional nature of a banking system restructuring, there is justification for curtailing the rights of interested parties to administrative review of such acts, at least to the extent necessary so as not to suspend the process of bank restructuring or liquidation of banks submitted to the bank restructuring regime. These restrictions on judicial authority should also apply to the civil courts, denying them the right to interfere in the bank restructuring process. In many countries, such restrictions are supported by the ability of interested parties to sue the bank restructuring agencies or the government for damages in civil court.

Exit and Sunset Provisions

Banking system restructuring legislation should prescribe precise criteria and procedures for the exit of rehabilitated banks from the jurisdiction of a BRC. Without these, the BRC might be subjected to unnecessary litigation by bank owners eager to regain control over their property. Even apart from the threat of litigation, exit criteria and procedures appear to be mandated by the goals of transparency and legal certainty.

The banking system restructuring law should have explicit sunset provisions that limit its life and that of the BRC to an expiration date, in order to avoid a situation in which this extraordinary regime would be used to restructure banks in circumstances unrelated to the banking crisis for which it was created. If necessary, the deadline can be extended by formal amendment of the legislation. These provisions should cover the transfer of any remaining assets and liabilities from the BRC and any associated asset management entity to the government.

However, there is an important disadvantage attached to such sunset provisions. Once the law has expired, its revival would require a full-fledged legislative procedure. In some countries, it takes a considerable period of time after a systemic banking crisis develops to draft and adopt suitable restructuring legislation, delaying restructuring of the banking system. Keeping restructuring legislation on the books would avoid such delays. This can be achieved, without risking that the restructuring law would be applied outside crisis situations, by limiting the effect of sunset provisions to a suspension of the law's operation, and by providing in the restructuring law that the law may be reactivated only under certain conditions pursuant to a simplified legislative process, such as a parliamentary resolution or a governmental decree issued with the advice and consent of the legislature.

Principal Objectives To Be Pursued by Law

In banking crises where existing regulatory and judicial resources are not equipped to administer a large number of failing banks, banking system restructuring should be carried out by a legally independent bank restructuring corporation (BRC) endowed with sufficient operational autonomy and financial resources. BRCs should be granted powers commensurate with their tasks. These powers should be clearly specified in the law.

The law should prescribe precise grounds and procedures for transferring failing banks to the banking system restructuring process and should provide that, upon transfer, the rights of existing bank owners and managers are vested in the BRC for the duration of that process. The law should require a restructuring plan for the banking sector as a whole and individually for each bank subjected to the banking system restructuring regime.

The law should contain precise exit criteria for reconstructed banks and a suitable sunset provision for the law itself.